Ruth Page

# God with Us

*Synergy in the Church*

SCM PRESS

0 334 027796 9

First published 2000
by SCM Press
9-17 St Albans Place, London N1 0NX

SCM Press is a division of
SCM-Canterbury Press Ltd

Set in 10.5/13 pt Postscript Linotype Sabon
Typeset by Rowland Phototypesetting Ltd,
Bury St Edmunds, Suffolk

Printed and bound in Great Britain by
Bibbles Ltd, Guildford and King's Lynn

# God with Us
## Synergy in the Church

# Contents

Part One: God with Us

Part Two: Synergy in the Church

# PART ONE

# God with Us

# I

# Then and Now

*What is the Church?; The Grave of God*. These are the titles of two books which stand next to each other on my shelves.[1] Their position was originally accidental, but since together they make a question and a threatened answer I have kept them as they are, as a kind of Awful Warning. How can the church avoid being 'the grave of God', in Nietzsche's words?

The books themselves were written in the late 1960s when optimism over the possibility of change overflowed from Vatican II into many churches. The Anglican Victor de Waal, whose book answers its title's question, was concerned about the institutional church and its structures. He pointed out how lightly Jesus himself sat to structures, but as for the church:

> Over the centuries its perennial instinct has been to tame the gospel and to contain God in its own categories. It has acted as if it knew exactly who Jesus was, has codified his teaching, and parcelled out his powers among its officials, while to the laity it has held out mainly his example of faithful obedience.[2]

Robert Adolfs, a Dutch Augustinian prior, hoped for change to escape the grave metaphor. He desired that the church should empty itself of its visible status and possessions, as Christ in the image of Philippians 2 emptied himself, and took on the form of a servant. But he could see the difficulties:

Whenever the Church automatically identifies herself with
her firmly established and highly respected external form
in society, then it is quite possible for it to appear as
though the loss of this form is the loss of the Church
herself.[3]

It is somewhat depressing to read these decades-old criticisms, hopes and prescriptions, for, although there have
certainly been some changes and a degree of loosening up in
the interim, institutionalized churches creak on, not visibly
emptier of anything except members. Is it worthwhile, then,
to attempt another book recommending change? I believe
that it is, particularly on account of three developments in
the culture of British society – that is, developments outside,
and not originating with, the churches, but which cry out for
a response.

The first of these is postmodernity in lifestyle and mindset,
that is, as general culture rather than in postmodernist philosophy. (I am following a sociological distinction between
postmodernity as a lived experience, and postmodernism as,
for instance, an intellectual movement in art, architecture
and literature.[4]) I shall discuss this more fully later, but here
it can be said that it will not do for the churches simply to
ignore or reject the attitudes and values of postmodernity,
drawing in their skirts as if to avoid infection. This is the
culture in which the church lives, in which its witness and
service take place, and if they take place in an attitude of
superiority on the part of the churches, with the desire simply
to remove people from their current culture, we may scarcely
hope to be heard, and will remain marginalized. The relation
between churches and the cultures in which and from which
they live will be a recurring theme throughout this book.

Another cultural change to which churches have given a
variety of responses is the often inchoate surge of desire for
spirituality. Whatever else that vague term may mean, and
again I shall return to it later, it expresses a sense of the self
which is not exhausted by scientific materialism, self-seeking

individualism or hedonistic consumerism. But few churches are making a concerted endeavour to encourage and promote spirituality. It is still as Rahner says: 'Living spirituality . . . has withdrawn in a singular way from the public life of the Church (considered sociologically) and has hidden in small conventicles.'[5] The number of conventicles may have grown since he wrote in 1974, but they are still as far as ever from affecting 'the public life of the Church'. Those churches with a tradition of spirituality have redoubled their efforts, yet these are still ancillary to the main structures and actions of the church. Those with no such tradition have scarcely put an exploratory toe into the water.

In both cases, however, serious spirituality could change the flavour, and even possibly the shape of the churches, for it progresses by networking rather than by centralized official pronouncements; its power lies in the attraction of small grass-roots groups rather than in the positions and possessions Adolfs wished to be rid of. Spirituality raises the possibility of alternative uses of power, and the church's understanding and use of power will again be a continuous strand throughout this book.

A third aspect of society which is too new to comment on in detail, but which gives a challenge to the church, is the Internet. Certainly in that unrestricted market-place cults and pornography may be found as well, but it is also an avenue open to the churches. A recent success was the website of the Church of Scotland's Society, Religion and Technology Project, which had an entry on cloning and its ethical issues even before Dolly the sheep was cloned. It was much visited from all round the world after that event.

But the effect of the Web may be much more fundamental. It is not locally circumscribed, as churches are, and is thoroughly democratic, being equally open to clergy and laity, to archbishops and deacons, to Roman Catholics and Pentecostals. The churches cannot control or regulate any but their own official pages. And although each person enters it privately, it is of its very nature interactive.

The electronic church is no longer territorial, no longer a parish or a synod or a diocese. The Cyber-community, or virtual community, knows no territorial demarcations and no hierarchies. The sense of pioneering and belonging to a new élite creates something like a new secular form of religious orders. They exist within the communicative streams of the electronic network in a certain opposition to the generally felt absence of communication structures in the traditional churches where horizontal interactivity has always been problematic.[6]

That account raises questions for the churches, including the freedom of the individual from church-inspired boundaries, but it does give a positive spin to Christian Internet use. Yet as far as sociological study of such use is concerned 'speculation far outstrips sound empirical research'.[7] Freedom from hierarchy and the joys of interactivity may indeed mean that new virtual communities of belief come into being. But investigation of New Religious Movements has shown that their recruitment is not from the virtual community, but comes through existing social networks and personal bonds.[8] In that case the attenuated bodiless presence of Internet users may work against relationships of enduring reciprocity.

That is the conclusion of Anne Wimberley as well, but she also makes the point that to counteract the attractions of cyberspace the value of presence must be evident. Attentive listening and responding, the making of relationships, become even more important. That insistence on the value of personal encounter and relationship is the line I shall be following in this book, and although I shall scarcely mention the Internet again, the emphasis is intended as a counterweight.

Because they are face-to-face environments, both our faith communities and seminaries have the potential for offering a vital communicative praxis that is qualitatively different from what people will continue to find in cyberspace.

In spite of the claims of virtual reality and artificial intelligence, and all that cyberspace promises, there is no substitute for embodied human presence in community.[9]

Postmodernity, spirituality, the freedom of the Internet: these are three of the current conditions which singly and together (postmodern spirituality on the Internet!) make it worthwhile to look again at the church, its theology and its social being, certainly for the sake of the church, but even more for the sake of God and God's work in the world.

But what is God's work, or, in other words, what theology underlies this description of the church? What is relevant here is not a full-blown ecclesiology, discussing such theologically technical questions as the manner of Christ's presence in the sacraments. Nor will there be a separate theoretical examination of the nature and purpose of the church, although perceptions of the church's purpose, and hence of its nature, occur throughout. Further, I am concerned that the theology and the practice described here should be interconnected. One may have elevated theological conceptions of the church which offer no insight or direction for the actual context of church living. It is equally possible to enlarge on church practice with only a nod in the direction of theology.

On the other hand, it is possible to have an understanding of God, and of what God was about in Christ, such that the church may celebrate it in its sense and form of worship, live it out individually and collectively, and put it into practice in all its activities. But the more elaborate the theology the more difficult it is to convey to the church at large. A theology for the church has to be simple enough yet deep enough, and compelling enough to be understood and interiorized personally and communally. Therefore, both the theology and the actions of the church will be explored on the basis of taking with full seriousness 'God with us'.

I shall take these three short Anglo-Saxon words 'God', 'with', 'us', and draw out their meaning, not in isolation from each other, but as two subjects joined by the full force of 'with', a word which precludes isolation. God in creation and salvation has chosen not to be 'God-alone', but 'God-with'; we in our families, communities, cultures are inescapably 'us-with', and I shall argue that whether we know it or not we are us-with-God. In other words we, others and God are always in relation on all sides, and the nature of that relation in its fullness is best defined by 'with'.

The first part of this book explores that understanding of relationship further. What kinds of relationship does God-with offer us? What possibilities of relationship are open to us-with? What is the promise of 'withness'? In the second part of the book that fundamental understanding is applied to all the relationships in which the church stands – worship, ministry, and many others inside, between, and outside individual churches, church families and other faith communities. For if a relationship defined by 'with' obtains between God and the church, its characteristics become the model for all relationships in which the church is involved, and a criterion for judging those relationships which at present fall short.

In writing this book I have been much influenced by seven years spent on the Central Committee of the World Council of Churches (WCC), an experience which, whatever its frustrations, certainly widens one's horizons on the variety of actual churches, their beliefs and practices, and the diversity of cultures, with their virtues and problems, in which they exist. Further, I served on the WCC's Commission on Mission and found contemporary thinking on mission far more vibrant than many home-directed ecclesiologies. It is in connection with mission that the real rethinking of relationships and redistribution of power has taken place – at least theoretically. The practice, I hear, is often less radical. But while that part of church life has changed its thinking, the home churches which once sent out missionaries have otherwise for the most part continued in the same old patterns of culture and power. There are, of course, other influences on this book, not least Rahner's thinking on grace and on the future shape of the church.

From time to time in this book boxes appear in relation to the text. These comment on the text with a story, an example, a further relevant quotation or, just occasionally, light relief. Their purpose is to draw the attention and underline a point.

# 2

# God-with

The evangelist Matthew, imbued with the Hebrew scriptures, finds a worthy name for Jesus in a prophecy from Isaiah (7.14): 'They shall name him Emmanuel, which means God with us' (Matt. 1.23). Knowing the effect of Jesus, perceiving him to be the Messiah, Matthew names him in continuity with his religious tradition. The God with whom Israel had covenanted had been among them, had been **for** them ('with' rather than 'against') in the person of Jesus.

Such an evaluation of Jesus is the foundation of belief in God-with and the grounds on which the eternal divine mystery beyond all human expression may be spoken of in finite words and images. Jüngel goes further with the suggestion that not only are we humans interpreting God, God is interpreting God for us in order to make the divine humanly interpretable: 'God's being-for-us does not define God's being, but certainly God in his being for us interprets his being.'[1] So for Christians the incarnation, the whole story of Jesus, reveals how God is for us, has always been and always will be: a God who has not abandoned creation, who in love is present in creation's contingent finitude and ambiguity, encouraging the good and condemning the bad, giving hope to the poor and disconcerting the rich, making possible present salvation and the forgiveness of sins. And the church is the place where this God is worshipped, while human life is understood in relation to these divine purposes.

To say that God is with us is to speak of an immanent God, here, now. That does not deny transcendence, God's existence above and beyond all things created. But what has happened in the past is that transcendence and immanence have been treated as if they were two different locations for God, one in the heavens and the other on earth. For most of Christianity's history God has been thought of almost exclusively as transcendent, 'up there' in glory: 'O worship the King, all glorious above'. But that view of an implicitly spatially transcendent God has a number of difficulties from today's perspective which I will only describe briefly here.[2]

First it means that God in heaven is normally absent from creation and has to make special arrangements to send the Son and the Spirit as it were across empty distance. They become the divine outreach from heaven to creation which is not God's dwelling place. Secondly, if God's home is thought of as vertically up in transcendence, all relations with God will be on a vertical axis of above and below, which in turn implies relations of command and obedience, of divine activity and passive human reception. That use of power is now perceived to be dehumanizing and unattractive among humans. It survives relatively unscathed only in the armed forces, and even there some modifications have been introduced.

In the third place, if God has to enter creation from without, a foreigner in creation, that will break the flow of history with its human and natural interactions over time. Such intervention removes creation's freedom to act and to be responsible for its actions and consequences. It is, further, acutely difficult to gain wide agreement on an instance of an intervention by God in contemporary or historical times, though certainly much of Israel's history is written in terms of such action. Finally, the amount of unabated innocent suffering, human and non-human, in a world loved by God, makes the occasional interventionist picture seem arbitrary.

Yet what this attribution of transcendence to God asserts cannot simply be dropped if God is to be God. A God without glory and with limited power is not the God of the Christian tradition. The cure for this dilemma, I believe, is to cease thinking as if transcendence and immanence were two different, almost competing locations for God. It is, in any case, unduly anthropomorphic to think of God in terms of locations. God, after all, is omnipresent: there is nowhere God is not. God is here, at my desk, as I write, and present wherever readers may be: yet God exceeds ever particular location. It is possible, therefore, to think of divine transcendence as radiating out infinitely from every local presence, so that God here, now, with us, is also and simultaneously the infinite God whom the heaven of heavens cannot contain. In the same way, the God whom we express in human language of a particular time and place exceeds all human language and culture. God may be, so to speak, immanent in the models we use, while also transcending them.

If God is, then, transcendently immanent, God has been 'with' creation from the beginning, needing no outreach or intervention to be present always with every creature rather than occasionally present with some. But that form of presence in turn affects the understanding of God's power and its use, with further consequences for the nature of God's actions and relationships.

Consideration of God's power should begin again with Jesus, since Jesus is our window on to God. What kind of power did Jesus exercise? The Gospels portray a man absolutely devoid of the trappings of power, who had not even a bed of his own. Yet people flocked to hear him. That shows, not the command of power from above, but the power of attraction alongside, the power of drawing people to himself. He rejected the more spectacular uses of power which occurred to him in his temptations and he sat lightly to the power of religious groups in his day, yet without setting himself apart from Judaism.

If that is how Jesus used power – not with spectacular displays of potency but with continuing, searching, local attractiveness, it seems quite reasonable to attribute that kind of power to God's immanence as well. God's omnipotence as sheer power is set aside in the divine self-interpretation and dealings with creation for an immanent attractiveness. And just as many people no doubt ignored Jesus, and some finally crucified him, so it is possible for people to ignore or reject the attraction of God who comes, not as king in the full panoply of omnipotence, not with an intervention to frighten and amaze, but in a carpenter's son from Galilee. In a striking picture John Robinson once described the chosen impotence of God:

> God's self-definition of power is terrifyingly simple – as simple and as terrifying as the cross. He has exposed the strong right arm by which he wills to curb the nations, and it is pierced with nails, stained with blood and riveted in impotence.[3]

And what of relationships? If God were to intervene with a public splash, the intervention would be enough to make the point and there would be no need to make or maintain relationships. Further, a king has only the most sketchy of relationships with his subjects. But for the immanent God who draws by attraction relationships become essential. There is therefore in place on God's side a relationship with every creature from the beginning, and the power of attraction exists to help creatures discover this. What God does, in that case, is not an action of intervention, but rather the making and maintaining of relationships.

I have found in trying to describe this that many men and some women cannot see the making of relationships as action at all. Yet relationships worthy of the name do not just happen and do not endure by chance. A marriage, as every counsellor knows, has to be worked at, and the same is true in their degree of less full-time relationships. But undoubtedly this is a different kind of action from that more traditionally attributed to God. For one thing a relationship makes one vulnerable to the other's suffering, or else there is inattention, misconstruing or loss, while macho action has none of these cares. A relationship is necessarily interactive; it has to respond to the other, and grant the other's freedom of response while remaining free to respond oneself. A powerful intervention overrules freedom and interaction. It astonishes and overawes rather than attracting.

The relationship on God's side with all creation is what Rahner describes as grace:

> Grace is God himself, his communication, in which he gives himself to us as the divinizing loving kindness which is himself. Here his work is really *himself*, as the one communicated. From the very first this grace cannot be conceived as separate from God's personal love and man's answer to it.[4]

Grace, he insists, 'is not rare'. It comes before, and makes possible, our responsive act of love.

And to the objection that all this is a far cry from notions of 'the mighty works of God', may be put Michael Northcott's redefinition of work:

> A new theology of work will involve an emphasis on creativity and service in which work is seen as essentially to do with the fostering of relationships, between rich and poor, between the sick and the healthy, between children and parents, between people and the land, and between sustainable technologies and genuine human needs.[5]

If that is human work, it is also surely divine work. All the characteristics of good relating may be attributed to God, even God's vulnerability to our inattention, misconstruing or wandering away. Yet God is always present, ready to interact with women and men, drawing them on into discovery of a deeper relationship.

But what kind of relationships does God-with, God present and drawing by attraction, have with men and women? There seem to me to be three which are all essential to human well-being and which describe a Trinity, not in terms of being or persons, but in terms of how God relates to us: a

Trinity from below, in the traditional way of expressing it, but really a Trinity alongside. Such a Trinity of relationships may be more comprehensible, more able to be accommodated into every-day Christian living than a Trinity described primarily as it is in itself (an immanent Trinity). That was Karl Rahner's hope as well:

> And thence the relationship between the 'immanent' Trinity and the Trinity in the economy of salvation could be rethought, and the highest mystery of the Christian faith be seen more clearly as a reality with which man has to do not only intellectually . . . but actually in his living of his life of grace.[6]

Thus, on the one hand, this is description of God in a three-fold relationship. But that is comprehensible, as Anne Primavesi insists, only because humans also live in a network of relationships and are not free-standing, lonely individuals.

> What God 'is' is indescribable, except in terms of a relationship described by a human being sustained by a knotwork of relationships within multiple environments . . . 'God', then, does not have a use, a function, outside a relational field . . . The function of my God-concept inheres in that network of relationships which includes those I have with God and with other human beings.[7]

But in this context it is not enough simply to say that one 'has' relationships. Relationships exist in different patterns which have to be analysed. First, relationships may be fixed or flexible. Human relationship with God requires something of both – both a God who is with us in all the changes and chances of this fleeting life, moving through them with us, and a constant God, fixed and unmoving, on whom we may rely. A fixed relationship is one over which we have no choice, but flexible relationships are freely entered into, change over time and may even be abandoned.[8]

## God as father, mother

The most obvious example of a fixed relationship in human life is that of a child with its parents, who were not chosen, but are part of the given of a child's life. In the contemporary diversity of human life there are, of course, exceptions to the straightforward parent and child relationship, and with increasing marriage breakdown such instances multiply. But the model is still recognizable. At their best parents are a source of security and give a sense of belonging. To a growing child they are an anchor in a contingent life and a home in an uncertain world. A perception of the quality of this relationship is given in Robert Frost's poem 'Death of a Hired Man', in which an old farm labourer has come back in a state near death to where he once worked. The farmer is grudging about his arrival and dismal on the subject of home:

> Home is the place where, when you have to go there,
> They have to take you in.

But his wife, with much greater warmth, replies,

> · I should have called it
> Something you somehow haven't to deserve.[9]

That not have to deserve it is the characteristic of love in the fixed relationship of parent and child. People may lose their good name, their money, their place in the world, and still be able to go home, where desert and success are not the entry criteria. The love that accepts the beloved in this way is unconditional: there are no hurdles to jump first. Conditional love, on the other hand, as its name implies, lays down conditions before it can be given. A parent who acts as if saying, 'If you keep off drugs, if you pass your exams, marry the right person, rise in your profession, or whatever, then I will love you,' is practising conditional love. Approval and acceptance will come only in response to approved and accepted actions. No doubt most parents have to use this kind of trade-off sometimes, but as a settled attitude it turns home into a place which has to be deserved, and may leave the child in a life-long struggle for parental approval, even after the parent's death.

Unconditional love, conversely, does not have to be earned, indeed cannot be earned by anything. It precedes and accompanies the loved one, however blind and partial that appears to a calculating world. It accepts rather than demands. Prodigal daughters and sons may indeed come home. It may be questionable whether unconditional love is possible for humans all the time. It is questionable whether it is even desirable for human relationships all the time, a matter I shall come to shortly. But those who have never experienced, at least sometimes, the rest, the security and the acceptance of such a home and parent have missed a very valuable experience.

Parental care is the most powerful and intimate experience we have of giving love whose return is not calculated (though a return is appreciated) . . . Parental love wills life, and when it comes, exclaims, 'It is good that you exist!' . . . Parental love nurtures what it has brought into existence, wanting growth and fulfilment for all. This agapeic love is revolutionary, for it loves the weak and vulnerable as well as the strong and beautiful. No human love can, of course, be perfectly just and impartial, but parental love is the best metaphor we have for imaging the creative love of God.

Salle McFague, *Models of God*, SCM Press 1987, p.103

The connection of this description of unconditional parental love with images of God as father or mother will be clear. God's love for erring humans is not deserved and cannot be earned. It is pure grace prior to everything else. We cannot earn it by works, though moralists of the faith keep trying to turn God's love into a merited response rather than an unmerited given. Even repentance and faith do not earn God's love. When it is said: 'If you repent God will forgive,' the forgiveness is made conditional upon the repentance and, in effect, women and men appear to trigger their own salvation by the 'work' of repentance.

The same rendering of God's love as conditional occurs also in some accounts of the atonement which begin by positing an unbridgeable gulf between God and humans created by sin. To believe that is to believe that God would acquiesce in the breaking off of relationship until some condition was met by Christ's death which at last enabled divine love to flow freely. In that interpretation God's love becomes conditional. But that kind of contract (if ... then ...) even between God and Christ goes against all that is said in Christianity of the constancy and gratuitousness of God's steadfast love. The existence of sin is undeniable: what is deniable is that this sin makes God withdraw relationship.

A relationship may be one-sided: known to one but not to the other. If unknown or unrequited human love is still love,

---

### Room at Home

Solidarity is expressed in a very particular way in Latin America, that is, through hospitality. There are many popular sayings that express very well the 'big heart' we Latin Americans have, usually manifested through women: 'where two eat three can eat', 'this place is like a mother's heart, there's always room for another', 'after the door has been closed there's still room for many inside', and many other sayings express this welcoming of others.

Silvia Regina, 'Reborn to Live', *Seeds of Living Hope*, Council of Churches of Latin America 1994, p.110

the relationship it forms with the loved one is still a relationship, though lacking the fullness of response. The same may be said of God's relationship with all humanity. On the human side, certainly, people may not respond, or even know of the relationship out of selfishness or ignorance. But the love of God is not withheld from the unaware until the conditions of Christ's atoning death and human responsive repentance are achieved. No one stressed that more compellingly than John McLeod Campbell, rebelling against the legal logic of hypercalvinism in nineteenth-century Scotland. He described God as 'yearning' over wayward children, and argued that forgiveness prompted the atonement rather than being the result of it.[10]

A very different theologian, Paul Tillich, describes one avenue of self-awareness which leads to the recognition of the home and parent quality of God's love. There are times when 'our disgust for our own being, our indifference, our weakness, our hostility and our lack of direction and composure have become intolerable to us'.[11] Grace in such a situation is to hear a voice saying: 'you are accepted . . . Do not try to do anything now; perhaps later you will do much. Do not seek for anything; do not preform anything; do not intend anything. *Simply accept the fact that you are accepted.*'

When I was younger I found that advice too passive. Again when 'God the Mother' began to be discussed I was initially opposed to it, not because the image was feminine, but because I thought one parental image for God was quite enough. I argued that parental images for God implied that Christians must be children when what was needed were mature, thoughtful, active adult Christians. There is still point in that argument which will be taken further below. But with the coming of age, responsibility and infirmity, and a greater sense of my own shortcomings, I am belatedly grateful that part of God's relationship with us is unconditional love. In situations of anxiety or unmeetable demand it is a release and a source of stability simply to accept that one is accepted – even, or especially, when one feels unacceptable.

We do not have to explain things to God, who understands it all already. We do not have to make anxious excuses for our behaviour, or brush ourselves up spiritually to be deserving of a welcome from the Father of every prodigal son or daughter. The relationship is fixed, unchanging, forever secure and dependable; in place before we even recognize our need.

## God as friend

Essential as the fixed relation with God is, it can never be sufficient for the Christian life, and therefore is insufficient as a description of God-in-relation. If acceptance were all, in all circumstances, then it would never matter what a person might actually do. There is no impulse towards growth to maturity in such a relationship. Further, since what people do is part of who they are, if they are loved no matter what they do, it is questionable whether they are being loved *as the people they are*. The love could be directed towards the category (my son/daughter, almost an extension of the self), and not to the person in all his/her indivuality and contingency. If that were all that could be said of God, then what would emerge would be an undiscriminating universal benevolence. So, while the benevolence, the loving-kindness, remains fundamental, there is more to relationship with God than that.

Some light on this problem may be shed by using the findings of Donald Winnicott, a child psychoanalyst, who distinguished two stages proper to the emotional, cultural, and, one might add, religious, growth of the individual. First there is the care-taker's holding of the infant, giving security and all the comforts of acceptance.[12] Such an infant, well held in bathing, feeding and so forth, is supported emotionally as well as physically, and protected from the anxieties of vulnerability. But then, Winnicott argued, should come a time of the growing child being given potential space.[13] The space is potential in that possibilities may be explored in it, and it is the young child's potential which begins to be exercised in it. The growing child is no longer in a state of absolute dependence, and the care-giver may begin to withdraw as the potential and the space increase. Winnicott held that this use of space and its potentialities gave rise to later creativity and cultural richness.

In human life these are serial stages as Winnicott describes them. Yet one could imagine that the mother, or other care-giver, could still offer the metaphorical 'holding' when needed even as the child progressed into adulthood. But a total simultaneity may be attributed to God, who both 'holds' and accepts humans whatever they have done, and 'lets be' so that they come to emotional, cultural and religious maturity.

I have described elsewhere God's action in creation as the letting be of the possibility of finite creatures.[14] Here it is important to maintain the distinction between 'letting be' and 'letting go'. Letting go implies dismissal, separation, abandonment. Letting be, on the other hand, implies the continual care and concern God has for those creatures to whom freedom has been given to discover the possibilities and the constraints of finite existence. This description of God's relating adds a different dimension to the parental model, therefore, in that while God remains the fixed 'home' we need, God is also the friend and companion of all the struggle of life. Thus there may exist with God a relationship which moves and responds to circumstances, is flexible in that sense rather than fixed, and whose reality in human life is chosen, entered into deliberately, rather than born into.

There are two forms of flexible relationships with other people and with God. One is private and personal, the other public and communal. I will describe the personal relationship under the metaphor of 'friend', and the public one as 'companion'. Companion seems to me to be a term that is warm, but not as enclosed as friend. The division is convenient and defensible, though the vagaries of actual English usage do not exactly correspond to it. One may, for instance, be friendly towards people who are not one's friends, while the Quakers, the Society of Friends, are as a group more like what I have called companions.

What is it to be a friend? By friend here I do not mean one of a range of people with whom one has more or less congenial relations, but one of the special, few intimates with whom one's thoughts, hopes and fears may be shared. Friends like each other, are drawn to each other, so friendship begins in attraction, but there is more to friendship than congeniality. Its two major characteristics are trust and honesty, which go together. There is the honesty which takes the risk of revealing oneself to another, laying oneself as well as one's circumstances open to her or him. The other is trusted with this self-disclosure and responds with similar openness and trust. Out of that shared giving and receiving a close bond is formed which sees both partners through good times and bad. Such friendship is an important concept for Moltmann:

> The new man, the true man, the free man is the friend. Existence *for* others within the regulation and functioning of the social order is necessary. But it is only legitimated as long as the necessity continues to exist. On the other hand existence *with* others, in unexacting friendliness, is free from necessity and compulsion. It preserves freedom because it unites receptivity with permanence. Friendship is the reasonable passion for truly human fellowship; it is a mutual affection cemented by loyalty. The more people begin to live with one another as friends, the more privileges and claims to domination become superfluous.[15]

Such friendships need not be claustrophobic. They grow out of each one's 'potential space' and will continue only if the space of each is respected by the other. A friend neither fills a role required by us nor exists simply to fill our need, but is someone with his/her own personhood. What emerges in a friendship, though it may never be explicitly articulated, is a mutual desire for the other's well-being and interests.

---

### Buddying

The befriending and support of people with an illness (usually at present AIDS or symptomatic HIV) on a one to one basis by trained volunteers. They are committed to confidentiality, regular contact, and helping people help themselves by keeping control of their situation. A buddy's activities might include chatting, cleaning, cooking, shopping and helping someone in their relationships with statutory and voluntary agencies. Asking for a buddy may mean acknowledging a diagnosis/prognosis and accepting a certain invasion of privacy, so buddies will need support, particularly if family and friends feel threatened by them. The relationship can continue or end by mutual agreement.

Malcolm Johnson, 'Buddying' in
*Dictionary of Pastoral Studies*, SPCK forthcoming

---

'I have called you friends' rather than servants says the Johannine Christ (John 15.5) to his disciples, and on that Moltmann comments: 'In the fellowship of Jesus they no longer experience God as Lord, nor only as Father; rather they experience him in his innermost nature as friend.'[16] God offers this close, personal one-to-one relationship as one of the needful divine ways of relating to humanity. It is offered and not imposed, showing God's trust in women and men to respond with trust of their own. This is a relationship which takes place in the midst of life as it is lived, in all its successes and failures, and is a place where honest self-examination of it all in God's presence may take place. Because God is friend one may batter on God's door with a request at any time, as in Luke's parable (Luke 11.5–10). But, on the other hand, stillness, openness in listening for God who desires the best for each one, is part of the exchange also. Private devotion, refreshment, counsel and encouragement are part of the total relationship with God. It is only when this one-to-one friendship is represented as the whole connection, as it has been in some evangelical quarters, that it becomes inadequate. It is, however, equally one-sided to be concerned over peace and justice issues to the exclusion of the intimate relationship God offers.

> The incarnation of God means: trust the nearness, because it is not void. Let go, then you will find; give up and you will be rich. The incarnation . . . is the promised beatitude. It can approach us without destroying us, it can tenderly enter our heart without breaking it asunder, it does not, like a crashing judgment, dash from distant heavens into the small sphere of our existence. No, it comes as grace saving us into its own freedom which it makes ours.
>
> Karl Rahner, *Grace in Freedom*,
> Burns and Oates 1969, p.200

Even in friendship the space in which each is him/herself remains, and this is true also of friendship with God. God is *with* us rather than taking us over – an unfriendly thing to do – and God remains distinct in divine freedom. But what is possible then, and only out of the space each has 'with' the other, is concurrence rather than submission. It is possible for a person to choose to concur, literally to run alongside, God, or it is possible to run in the opposite direction entirely. Submission is for slaves; friends share in uncoerced concurrence.

What is made possible in God's offer of friendship is the presence of God with each individual, treasuring each, trusting each, looking for trust in response; God responding to each with encouragement or warning. Thus human faith is kept vital and love existential in the midst of personal pains and pleasures, and human friendship in its turn becomes a sacred act.

When, for example, a concrete human being . . . expresses genuine personal love for another human being, it always has a validity, an eternal significance and an inexpressible depth which it would not have had but that such a love is so constituted as to be a way of actualizing the love of God as a human activity springing from God's own act.[17]

---

Christ minds: Christ's interest, what to avow or amend
There, eyes them, heart wants, care haunts, foot follows
    kind,
Their ransom, their rescue, and first, fast, last friend.

Gerard Manley Hopkins, from 'The Lantern out of Doors'

---

## God as companion

This form of relationship moves from the God who cares for me, though that specialness is true of each individual, to God who cares for the unemployed, those with HIV/AIDS, the people of the debt-ridden, drought-or-flood-ridden countries of the south, and so forth. God companions all these in the full scope of their circumstances as well as valuing each individual. Each individual in any case, although special as a self, lives in the midst of these larger movements, and in a network of relationships. What I have called companionship Moltmann calls 'open friendship', meaning one which moves away from all overtones of exclusivity, both on the personal level (prizing *my* relationship with Jesus above anything else going on in the world), and the exclusivity of peer friendship, the friendship restricted to 'one of us'. He notes how unlike Jesus that is:

Had he abided by the peer principle, he would of necessity have had to stay in heaven. But his incarnation and his fellowship with sinners and tax-collectors breaks through the exclusive circles. For this reason Christian friendship also cannot be lived within a closed circle of the faithful and pious, of peers in other words, but only in open affection and public respect of others.[18]

Companionship has long seemed to me the best current metaphor for God and Christians at work together in the world with the affection and respect Moltmann invokes.[19] Companions literally share bread, as in the eucharist. They also may share a journey, a task or a diversion. Friends are 'with' each other in the closeness of intimacy, but the 'with' of companionship is a wider sharing and alignment with others, even others very different from oneself. The ideal space of companionship is that in between crowding the other and remaining distant and aloof. Companions are more than a fortuitous aggregation of isolated individuals, such as one might find on the London Underground, for some attraction must have drawn them together. There must be some com-

---

In 1988 I found my nerves jolted by a bus journey from Tiberias to Jerusalem – especially because the majority of passengers appeared to be heavily armed Israeli soldiers. One such sat beside me, but since he spoke little English, and I less Hebrew, the rather tense journey continued in silence.

At Jericho there was a 'comfort stop', after which the young serviceman re-boarded the bus carrying two cold drinks and a packet of biscuits. He passed one can of juice to me and, breaking open the biscuits, gave me half the packet.

The rather intimidating stranger had literally become a 'companion' – one who shares bread. For the first time I saw him as a fellow human being caught up in a situation which, in all likelihood, he did not completely understand and to which there appears no obvious solution.

W. McLaren in *Life and Work*, August 1997

monality of interest, character or purpose. Further, there is both dependence and independence in the relationship: dependence in the way one is influenced by one's companions, and independence in that however much the influence one remains responsible for what one does.

God's relation with creation at large, human and non-human alike, is one of companionship. Again this is a relationship, like friendship, offered to creation by God, who lets be, but does not let go. But this is a relationship concerning what one does in the world, rather than one's spiritual state; it leads, not only to concurrence with the divine, but also to synergy, the pooling of energies, divine and human, to bring about God's desire for creation. As that desire may be expressed in terms of freedom and love[20] the aims of companionship with God are the enlargement and flourishing of creaturely freedom and love. The dependence and independence of companionship remain in evidence, a dependence on divine influence, but an independence in taking actual decisions and actions in an ambiguous and finite world. These work together in the relationship, for 'When God is known as companion, we are not only responsive and responsible *to* him, we are responsive and responsible *with* him.'[21]

Human work is thus influenced and energized by divine desires for creation's well-being. But that gives no blueprint for what in particular instances is to be done:

> God is not the map-maker who designed the route, and then observes our own progress; he is not even the guide who has been that way many times, for in a changing world each way is different. But he is the companion of eminent experience and loyalty, whose wisdom is an ever present help.[22]

Because this book is largely concerned with what the church might be or do in this changing age the second part will be an elaboration of what companionship might mean in these times. Since that is God's way of relating to the world at large in all its vicissitudes, it will also be the way for the church to go, exploring the meaning of 'with' in all the situations it faces. But that form of withness would be sterile if it had not also the security of Father and the intimacy of Friend to give it depth and staying power. So while these relations will be less mentioned in what follows, they are presupposed as what renews and strengthens the possibility of companionship.

Images of life as a journey or of the church as the pilgrim people of God are illuminated by divine-human roles of companionship, for in any pilgrimage the quality of hopeful travelling is as important as the intention to arrive.[23]

About a dozen people had gathered ... Between them they faced chronic problems of alcohol and drug abuse, mental illness and social inadequacy. We sang the well-known chorus: 'Bind us together, Lord'. It was never my favourite; in fact I find its sentimental longing for cosy fellowship nauseous. The final verse which suggests that 'We are God's chosen', usually implying a fresh-faced gathering of worthy people, I find particularly off-putting. However this time as I sang these words I found myself wondering whether this motley group of homeless and mentally distressed could be God's chosen. The answer came without hesitation: yes they were most certainly God's chosen, and for the first time in my life I had a clue about the vastness of God's grace.

Ann Morisy, *Beyond the Good Samaritan*, Mowbray 1997; reprinted in *Urban Theology: A Reader* ed M. Northcott, Cassell 1998, p.240

## The Trinity

This has been a perspective on the Trinity from below, from how people experience God-in-relation expressed in human models of relationship. I have described relations of acceptance in unconditional love; of close personal intimacy with its discovery of honesty, trust and concurrence; of fellowship in wider concerns of justice, peace and the flourishing of creation. These are very different relations, and no one human could fulfil them all to each. But as they are all necessary in relating to God, they form an approach to comprehending in life that self-differentiation in God called the Trinity. It is one God at work in all of them, but the working is very different. One (Father-child) relationship is fixed, unchanging, with human activity unnecessary; the others take place in, and respond to, changing circumstances. Two are personal between each human being and God (Father, Friend); one involves the whole way creation goes. All are necessary in divine-human relationships, and in view of the variety, if the Christian faith were not already trinitarian, something like the ancient doctrine would have to emerge.

In this book, however, I have not assigned 'persons' of the Trinity to God's relationship with the world, although as I have described them they could fairly easily fit into a form of the roles of Father, Son and Spirit. It has always been said that the works of the Trinity in relation to creation are indivisible. Nor would I wish any overtones that 'Father' and 'home' are somewhere remote while 'Friend' and 'Companion' are here below. God is simultaneously immanent and transcendent, and equally simultaneously Parent, Friend and Companion. The differentiation at any point concerns human need rather than some division of relation within the being of God. I have therefore continued to use the word 'God' on its own for the divine side of the relationship. But all of God-in-relation is involved in creation and salvation and thus in the continuance of unconditional acceptance, underlying befriending and challenging companionship at all times.

# 3

# Us-with

Who are we, with whom God has these relationships? In pluralist, postmodern times that is almost an unanswerable question, except in terms of diversity. There is diversity even in the degrees of postmodernity people 'flow' with. They may still adhere to more or less of modernity, while a few have chosen to return to, or may never have removed from, aspects of premodernity (before the Enlightenment). Yet as postmodernity is the new thing the churches have to grapple with, it is that aspect I shall describe. In 1974 Karl Rahner could already perceive the changes taking shape:

> We are living in the age of the mass society where authority is regarded as merely functional, and in which, by an odd juxtaposition, freedom and interdependence have become key concepts . . .
> We are living in a world where society is pluralistic; that is, in which, even in the individual historical sphere, there is no longer a society which sets up concrete guidelines for all its groups.[1]

Postmodernity may, of course, be simply another phase the Western world is passing through, and descriptions based on it may come to seem as erroneous as J.A.T. Robinson's confident assertion in 1952 that interdependence had arrived, so that 'the age of individualism is over', and again in 1960 that 'the days of *laissez-faire* are gone for ever'.[2] We have recently emerged from the time of the 'me-generation' and a government concerned to re-establish *laissez-faire*. So nothing is certain. Martin Palmer regards this as a time of unrest after which things may settle down again:

> [M]ajor changes in religious thinking are actually taking place, and before a new orthodoxy can arise, variety becomes the flavour of the month and there contend 'a hundred schools', as the Chinese put it.[3]

Yet to describe the 'us' with whom God is in relation now, at the point where the church is and acts at the moment, post-modernity has to be taken with full seriousness.

This is not capitulation to the *Zeitgeist* of the kind Avery Dulles suggested:

> [A]ny restructuring of the Christian ministry should be something more than a reflection of the contemporary Zeitgeist. It should take full cognizance of the biblical roots and of the special mission of the church.[4]

That is undoubtedly true. But the biblical roots of the church and its ministry are so various that everything from foreshadowed episcopacy to congregationalism to charismatic outpourings may be found therein.[5] (That is why there is no separate section on the church in the Bible in this book: the only conclusion to be drawn from a study of the New Testament is that the early church flourished in a variety of forms.) Dulles cites the special mission of the church as another reason for not conforming to the *Zeitgeist*. Certainly the church always witnesses to God's saving love which transcends all places and times. Yet the message of that love has to be heard in all places and times. It has to be clear that this message is *for us*, that God is with *us*, here and now, and not as the residue of an earlier manifestation. For that some accommodation with the *Zeitgeist* has to be made, although how far one should go is always a fruitful area for disagreement. Awareness of the importance of the context of the church's existence is as necessary as it is difficult. As Rahner once more comments on the incalculability of the future: 'neither a promised land nor a final catastrophe will soon take away from us the burden and the dignity of a continuing pilgrimage through history'.[6]

What, then, is this context? It is almost indescribable, for postmodernity as an ethos is protean. Change and unpredictability are two of its most salient characteristics. A few generalizations may however be made. Whereas the sciences had contributed to the mind-set of modernity by nurturing notions of evidence, predictability and the control of nature, scientists in the wake of the atomic bomb, noxious pesticides and other scares have lost their unquestioned authority, while chaos theory which investigates dynamic open systems has to some extent changed its character. Further green movements see nature as something with its own life and value rather than as a resource or a tool for human use and benefit. The organization of industrial society, and the nuclear family which suited that means of production, are in decline or have gone, to be followed by the rise and fall of smaller, technological or service industries, and the greatest possible range of permutations of family and couple arrangements, with working wives the norm rather than the exception.

Consumerism is required by a global economy and is encouraged by ubiquitous marketing to become part of people's self-description ('I shop, therefore I am'). Freedom of choice has become a prime value, however circumscribed it may be in reality, so allegiances such as those to the church have splintered into more or less temporary adherence to many different groups with no overriding loyalty. Single issues set protesters on fire rather than the older class frictions, and they contribute to the search for an identity which is no longer simply given. Politics and politicians caught in the media's glare have lost their automatic legitimacy while the nation state with its enlargement to Europe and participation in globalization has become a good deal less than sovereign. Although islands of familiar modernity remain, much seems to be in flux, while old certainties with their beliefs or ideologies are widely perceived to have lost their credibility. Social Science has contributed to this situation by its description of the degree of social construction in conceptions of reality, including the expression of beliefs, which regularly came complete with a narrative which justified their power over people.

Nevertheless, as Rahner saw, and Robinson hailed somewhat prematurely, the perception that we are interdependent is increasing. That is due to global trade and improved communications, including all media, and also to a re-evaluation of non-human nature. Humans cannot simply control nature, or use it for their own immediate ends, or they will make their home planet uninhabitable. Again, while in some businesses straightforward internal competition or top-down authority is still practised, there is an increasing emphasis on bonding, partnership, synergy. And in Rahner's 'odd juxtaposition' the emphasis on interdependence sits alongside the demand for freedom of choice in everything from schools to supermarkets to belief-systems. What comes over to people as demand or imposition is fiercely resented. Deference is out of fashion. If interdependence encourages the 'with' of us-with, and is an inescapable feature of life at large, the emphasis on freedom means that people wish to choose whom they will be 'with' as far as they can.

Where does the church fit into this picture? As an institution it could be described as remaining firmly in modernity with only a few individual postmodern fringes. The historian Will Storrar has analysed this situation in relation to the Church of Scotland, but his analysis holds with few changes for all mainline churches. He argues that the widely accepted account of the church's recent past is misleading.

> The argument goes that since the Enlightenment in the eighteenth century we have become a more secular, rational and scientific culture, and in that more inhospitable and hostile environment the churches have withered and Christian belief has evaporated.[7]

> Modernist Christianity, in keeping with modernist intel-
> lectual endeavour, is greatly interested in the truth. This is
> the fundamental reason for the existence of so many
> denominations, and the doctrinal debate which has driven
> several hundred years of definitions and argument ...
> Truth is out there, and each group claims that it has the
> franchise on it. This form of religious belief could only
> have emerged within modernism, in which truth is objec-
> tive, rational, dispassionate, coherent and Platonically
> eternal.
>
> M. Riddell, *Threshold of the Future*, SPCK 1998, p.112

Against this Storrar argues that the church in fact moulded
itself well to the post-Enlightenment conditions of modernity. On the one hand it became an institution in the modern
form with a centralized headquarters, a central collection
and distribution of funds, a bureaucracy and a clutch of
committees, with a heavy emphasis on mass membership. Its
theologians grappled bravely with modern issues of scientific
rationality from biblical criticism to the theory of evolution.
Thus modernity shaped the form and interests of the modern
church. It was, quite properly, responding to the conditions
of its time. Numbers were certainly declining slowly, but it
is precisely in the 1960s, when the postmodern ethos began
to make itself felt, that the Kirk began to lose significant
numbers while traditional campaigns were not noticeably
successful in recouping them. Storrar concludes:

The Church of Scotland is not so much declining as changing. It is the culture to which it has been wedded for over
two hundred years which is declining, modernity itself.
And so it is experiencing the decline of modernity, of
which its own institutional decline is an integral part, as a
time of loss and grieving ... Like individuals in the grieving process the institutional and ecclesiastical culture of

the Kirk are responding to their loss with numbness and bewilderment, anger and denial, bargaining and depression. The Church of Scotland shows little sign yet of reaching the stage of acceptance in the grieving process; of being ready to work through that loss as a process of necessary and ultimately healing change, leading to a new role and identity in Scottish society.[8]

The Church of Scotland is certainly not alone in this recognition. John Tiller points out that as early as 1970 Valerie Pitt reported to the Church of England that it might be identifying itself with a dying culture. Commenting on that Tiller writes:

That, it seems to me, is the greatest danger offered in the communal [parishes in a local community] model today. It really has more to do with our cultural past than our religious present. With which particular culture are we identifying? Is it a culture that is in principle nostalgic, related to the small, close-knit communities of the past?[9]

Tiller's doubts about past ready-made communities, such as those which once flourished in mining villages (though rural communities still do exist) may be right. To think in terms of such set groupings would be nostalgic for a Britain that scarcely exists today. And to the extent that parish boundaries still reflect such bygone communities they may be a hindrance rather than a help. But in a time of many ad hoc congregating, such as the Trekkies of *Star Trek*, the possibility of forming non-traditional communities remains, and Tiller himself advocates an associational basis.

Storrar mentioned the need for grief at the passing of the modern paradigm, but that grief should be tempered by consideration of the ambiguity of the values which the connection between the church and modernity wrought. On the one hand some may lament the loss of 'civic virtues' underwritten by the churches: 'duty, self-sacrifice, honour, service, self-discipline, self-improvement, civility, fortitude, courage, diligence and patriotism'.[10] These are all potentially noble, though one may wonder whose interests they tended to serve in practice.

For on the other hand there is this outcry from Margaret Kane:

> In our urban/industrial society a few models: Lord, Master, King, Father dominated our conception of God. These models have seemed to make sense of and validate our particular kind of society . . . [I]t is clear that religion is a factor in supporting the values of industrial society: hierarchical organization, obedience to external authority, paternalism, dependence on the benign domination of the *male* 'Father' figure . . . The qualities these models stress contradict the most creative insights of today: participation, the responsibility and power of human beings, human solidarity, the equality of men and women.[11]

Storrar himself in that article does not go much further in rethinking the church's role in postmodernity than to insist that a church can no longer be measured by the number of its members. But the next important concerns are clearly with the shape and nature of a church in contemporary society. I believe Storrar to be right, so that there is no point in either making a few adjustments to churches as they are, nor continuing as at present and hoping for the best. God is with us in the insecurity of change, companioning us, offering us synergy and with the divine energies as ways are explored to communicate a gospel that will be heard in our current upheaval.

The British, or the West in general, may gain more encouragement by the thought that we are not alone in having to rethink the theology and practice of the church. In South Africa, for instance, many church people are struggling to move from a theology of resistance to a theology of reconstruction to keep up with what is happening in their society.

In the 1880s my Cree grandmother worked as a young woman in a Presbyterian residential school at Round Lake, Saskatchewan, near the reserve where her father lived. Although he always supported the sun dance, the mentality of those who converted as Presbyterians was that you had to choose to live either in the indigenous world or the white world. Since the buffalo were gone the pressure was to live in the white agricultural world. You wore Western dress; you opted to be Christian and 'civilized'. The predominant ideology and theology seemed to be a complete fusion of Christianity with the Anglo-European way of life.

Janet Silman, *The First Nations: A Canadian Experience of Gospel-Culture Encounter*, WCC Publications 1995. p.16

Since their theology must now address everyone, and deal with the ambiguities of power, new skills have to be acquired and a new openness learnt: 'To play a role in conflict resolution [the churches of South Africa] must listen to *all* sides in seeking to promote reconciliation.'[12] There is movement, too, in countries which were evangelized by the West, where Western thought-forms and conceptions were imposed on local cultures along with the gospel. Converts were called on not only to leave their former religions, but also their cultures as outward expressions of those religions, even though that might mean the shattering of tribal loyalties and community customs, and the dissolution of age-old family patterns. But, as Ariarajah notes, as one cannot exist outside any culture so 'this resulted in the convert's taking on the culture of the person who converted him to the Christian way of life'.[13] It was the coming of independence which produced the new situation with which churches are still grappling.

The foreignness of the churches in Asia and Africa and the accusation that they were the vestiges of colonial

powers set these churches into fresh thinking about their
indigenous culture . . .

The most striking image, popularized by Asian thinkers
like D.T. Niles, was that of a potted plant. The gospel had
been brought to the nations as a plant, with the pot being
western culture. This may have been inevitable, but now
the plant must be transferred into Asian or African soil,
so that it might strike deep roots and draw nourishment
from it.[14]

The rest of the world has been thinking long and hard
about the relation between culture and religion. At the 1975
Assembly of the WCC in Nairobi a ringing affirmation
concerning the equality of cultures was made:

[N]o culture is closer to Christ than any other culture.
Jesus Christ restores what is truly human in any culture
and frees us to be open to other cultures . . . He offers us
liberation from attitudes of cultural superiority and from
self-sufficiency. He unites us in a community which transcends any particular culture.[15]

On the British scene that affirmation holds between the culture of modernity – the Western culture which was so widely
exported – and the culture of postmodernity which we have
yet to think through. We have behaved as if we thought
modern Western culture was here forever. But now, to revert
to D.T. Niles' image, the gospel is pot-bound in its modern
form, and requires replanting into postmodern soil, no
matter how unpromising that may seem to some.

For the purpose of this digression into other cultures and
the gospel has been to point out that we live in a time of
world-wide ferment of thought and belief about the contemporary, indeed localized presence of God with us. 'Christ
Would be an African Too' is the sub-title of John Pobee's
WCC pamphlet on West Africa. Would Christ be post-

modern? Very probably. So if all that explosion of imme-
diacy is happening elsewhere with change and variety endorsed, it would be a kind of failure of nerve if such
rethinking were to be absent in the West, so that inherited
forms and traditions were simply continued because they
were there and churches lacked the spiritual energy to
respond to the present. Pobee writes that the gospel and
culture debate 'should be rooted in commitment to the conviction of one Creator God whose creation is manifold and
pluriform'. In other words this is commitment to a God who
enjoys diversity. So the manifold and pluriform nature of
postmodern Britain is not in itself to be deplored. And the
task, says Pobee, 'is multi-faceted – theological, pastoral,
liturgical, ritual, didactic and spiritual'.[16]

The South African David Bosch invokes the notion of
creative tension for such a time as this:

> [B]oth the centrifugal and the centripetal forces in the
> emerging paradigm – diversity versus unity, divergence
> versus integration, pluralism versus holism – will have to
> be taken into account throughout. A crucial notion in this
> regard will be that of *creative tension*: it is only within the
> force field of apparent opposites that we shall begin to
> approximate a way of theologizing for our own time in a
> meaningful way.[17]

There will certainly be tension as the church changes, but it
seems rather optimistic to call it 'creative'. Of Bosch's three
opposites I am more concerned in this book for the church to
cope with diversity than to work at its unity; to see what
divergence is possible among Christians rather than integrat-
ing it all together; to enjoy pluralism (and to believe that God
enjoys pluralism) rather than subsuming variety under a
holistic paradigm. In a way that emphasis is one-sided, but
given where churches are at present, in their old paradigm
and losing numbers and confidence, it is the new rather than
the old situation which has to be encouraged. Once convinced

that change, often already underway, is necessary and may be experimented with, perhaps a synthesis of Bosch's 'apparent opposites' may be possible.

Robin Greenwood comments on the local incarnation of Christianity in England, but the principle would hold equally for the Indians of the Andean highlands and the Maoris of New Zealand as well as for the people of the Leeds housing estate which was principally in his mind. In a good ecclesiastical sense, 'we are not alone'.

> Christianity can only become an incarnated and authentic way of living when it builds upon, and makes sense of, ordinary life, here and now. Although any culture must stand under the judgment of Christ, the kingdom that the church must proclaim is to be worked for on earth, as in heaven. This means that the Christian community should not be allowed to become a shelter from the storm, a place of security or respectability in which to escape the dreariness and pain of human responsibilities and relationships.[18]

The evenhandedness of that statement including affirmation and judgment is echoed in Will Storrar's comment, particularly apposite when the advent of a Scottish Parliament has intensified Scottish national feeling, with repercussions in England:

> As those who find their true identity in Christ, our approach to our own national identity will always involve his three-fold response of affirmation, opposition, conversion: identification, separation, transformation.[19]

These are fine principles, whose value is not diminished by the church's frequent disagreement on what exactly is to be affirmed, opposed or transformed.

So us-with are various, variously seeking our identity, yet linked in interdependence. That is the human end of the relationship with God. Simultaneously, however, in Avery Dulles's words:

> Wherever the grace of Christ is present it is in search of a visible form which adequately expresses what it is.[20]

As Christ himself was the visible form of God's grace, so the church, when it has an adequate visible form, may be a sacrament of that grace, while a sacrament, Dulles insists, has a dynamic, event character. For the invisible grace to become visible, anywhere from West Africa to West Hartlepool or West Lothian, it requires a form which will embody it, however fallibly, and convey it to others. But there is always the danger that the form may make the grace (that grace which called it into being) invisible. The grace of God, which I have expressed in relationships, may be relied upon –

---

Church that could be envisioned on the basis of Jesus' parable of the good Samaritan is not something that is given, but something that happens. It happens when those women and men carrying heavy burdens are given rest, when release is proclaimed to the captives, sight restored to the blind, freedom won for the oppressed ... The church that comes into being in this way is a movement, not an institution, a community of persons, not a hierarchy of clergy, the bearer of the good news and not a structure erected on power and privilege. In contrast, a religious establishment that does not happen in this way, even though adorned with pomp and glory, boasting of long and illustrious traditions, celebrating Christian festivals with meticulous observance of church calendar, is not church.

Choan Seng Song,
'Doing Christian Theology with Jesus in Asia',
*International Review of Mission*, Jan–April 1995, p.120

sure as parent, close as friend, challenging as companion. But
if we rest too comfortably on our traditions – our Reformed
heritage, the glories of the Anglican Communion, the genius
of Methodism, the world-wide, age-long spread of the
Roman Catholic Church, or whatever – then we treat God's
grace as a thing of the past, now settled. But God's relationship is here, now, with us. The question before all the
churches is: 'Given the culture in which you live, what visible
form is the grace of Christ seeking now?'

## The importance of relative relativism

The description of us-with has been full of references to
change and difference, to letting a thousand flowers bloom in
the Christian church as a whole. Implicit in that is the notion
that no one human version can encompass all truth which
may then be extended to or imposed on others. That demon-
strates in the Christian domain the passing of the notion of
any human expression of an absolute truth and certainty.

In modernity it was once believed, for instance, that his-
torians could arrive at describing the past as it really was, as
if the past were not a variety of things to a variety of people.
Further, scientists were believed to be progressing further up
a single ladder of knowledge. Real knowledge was enshrined
in scientific empiricism, and only to the extent that other
ventures could use the same criteria and methods did they
appear to be sound. That was as true of theology as of any
other subject, and it came under criticism where it appeared
to fail. At the same time, though in a different field, moral
absolutes like goodness were believed to be universal in their
proper conception and application.

But historical study itself has shown that this 'Enlightenment project' was the self-understanding of a particular time
and place (the West, eighteenth to twentieth centuries) which
was so successful on its own terms that it was thought to be
absolute and universal. It is entirely understandable that
missionaries and other colonizers would judge other coun-

tries by its terms and wish to extend its perceived benefits. But history cannot give one single true account of the past, and it was when scientific study was examined historically that it too was seen to embody change and difference. That does not invalidate either historical or scientific study, but it does relativize them to the contexts in which they are done.

---

### Whose History?

When I was at Harfleur in Normandy some years ago, the church bells rang out in honour of the 'hundred men of Harfleur' who in the Hundred Years' War had pushed an English army back into the sea. I had never heard of them; but then neither had my French hosts heard of Crécy, Poitiers and Agincourt!

Victor de Waal, *What is the Church?*,
SCM Press 1969, p.84

---

The current truism is that nothing will be seen unless one has a point of view, while any point of view, being localized, will also limit and shape what can be seen. What is seen or known is relative to the point from which it is seen. That relativism has caused shock in many places. It appears to license the 'anything goes' attitude, and fear of that has been enhanced by playful deconstruction of older certainties.

But the choice does not have to be between holding grimly on to views of ascertainable truth universally agreed, together with moral absolutes on the one hand, and a descent into total relativism on the other. No one can, in fact, live in complete relativism, whatever theoretical views may be held. Everyone has at least preferences, and may arrive at logical argument and moral priorities which seem the best currently available.

What we live in, then, is a relative relativism, in which much is held as decided, though open to change if something more persuasive appears. Earlier, in a much more extended discussion, I called this relativity, but perhaps the other term is better.[21] It is also coherent. If everything is relative, then even relativism is relative. Relative relativism does not remove people's firm adherence to what they think is true or right, nor does it remove their freedom to recommend these views to others. Kate Rawls gives a good example:

> The contention that racial hatred is wrong is not just personal preference but a claim that can be argued for – and against. If values were subjective preferences such arguments would not make sense.[22]

What relative relativism requires is only recognition that there will be genuine, not simply unenlightened, differences in viewpoint and values, so that the one recommended has to attract in the midst of difference, and may indeed learn and change from that difference.

No absolutes may be claimed, but one thing may seem more persuasive than another, and may be believed and followed. Relative relativism is the mature attitude of people who have come to some conclusions about *their* values and priorities as well as mere preferences, and so may exercise them in the midst of difference. If what is true or right for one, or a group, is attractive to others acceptance will spread. Nevertheless, as contexts are different, the working out of that truth and rightness may well differ from place to place.

Relative relativism, therefore, puts into practice on a human and finite plane much the same way as I have described God working. Just as with God pronouncement from on high is seen to have given way to a conception of immanent persuasion, so, with humans, simple, but actually time-bound, proclamations of the truth have given way to the persuasion of attractiveness. And again, the perception that God enjoys the diversity of creation over time is an encouragement to enjoy the diversity of religious expression now.

It is not, then, a case of 'anything goes' and nothing may be justified. Justification will be made in terms of the point of view, the point of belief. That is part of human finitude. But that expression of belief may yet draw others to it. And in the openness of relative relativism and the capacity of people to change, one may find others' expression of faith attractive as well, and incorporate that within one's understanding and practice.

A further matter raised by postmodernism is the question of 'presence'. A theology based on 'God with us' is clearly making much of divine presence. Yet in postmodernism there is frequent scepticism of the facile presentation or representation of, for instance, authorial presence. When that scepticism is applied to theology it issues in negative theology (what God is not), finding at best only a trace of God which would be wiped out if it were put into language, or, in Blanchot's phrase, 'a non-absent absence'. Although Rowan Williams does not quite share this view he expresses it well:

> [T]o speak of God is to try to put a face upon that which haunts language – what is over the shoulder, round the corner, what is by stipulation not capable of being confronted, being *faced*.[23]

This expression of the elusiveness of presence is in many ways a good counter-balance to my own confident assertions of God with us. It is a reminder that God is never contained in any description. Yet disillusionment with the pretentions of having caught any presence, let alone the presence of God, need not, it seems to me, require the swing to the opposite pole of absence, even a nearly-there absence. That shows the same kind of excessive reaction to the loss of total certainty as the swing to total relativism.

What the reminder of elusiveness may require instead is more humility in representation, and a sense that all such representations are part of a continuing dialogue (a dialogue, not a pronouncement) rather than a finished article. Thus, although this book endeavours to give a coherent basis for belief and practice in the presence of God, its assertions are bounded on the one hand by the mystery God is, and on the other by those who would differ on its theological or practical recommendations. It thus becomes an input into a dialogue on God and the church, written as persuasively as I may. I have 'captured' neither God nor theological truth. It would be hubris to think otherwise.

Another area in which relative relativism has something to offer is in the matter of 'metanarratives', 'grand narratives', 'master narratives', those stories which are told by groups, including Christian groups, to place and explain themselves in relation to the past and the present, and to give a set of values for living. Postmodern philosophers have often rejected such narratives, suspecting, often quite rightly, that they existed to justify those in power and served to disempower the 'other'. Undeceived fragmentation, living without a cover story, was, they believed, better than succumbing to the control and the divisiveness of a narrative. Further, no master narrative could ever cover every contingency, and thus would at some point be found wanting, 'found out'.

The question whether there can be a Christian grand narrative, an overarching story of why we are what we are, is highly important on its own, but gains further point from the way in which the vacuum in narratives has allowed the market simply to represent everything as yet another commodity or range of commodities in what Lieven Boeve has called 'the economizational narrative'. Religions in that case exist only in that they meet a demand:

> In so far as the religious need lives in the individual and the community – more generally described as a longing for harmony, consolation, wholeness – the market place fills the gap with an offer of religious and para-religious products which purport to satisfy this need.[24]

But what are churches to do in face of this construction of their being and aims? Their most evident response, which Will Storrar charitably called part of the grieving process, is the reiteration of past positions.

> Through a suspension of dialogue with postmodern culture, churches fall back to their formerly held positions and call believers to obedience based on their own authority [or tradition].[25]

But that, as Boeve points out, simply adds confirmation to the 'primacy of arbitrariness' in the culture. He takes his example from his own church, but all churches which have simply opposed current practices fall into the same dynamic:

> When . . . the Roman Catholic hierarchy excludes women from the priesthood, continues to forbid the use of contraceptives, and silences critics who belong to its own community, this regularly appears on the front pages of newspapers and in various news bulletins on radio and television, as well as inciting indignant reactions from both believers and unbelievers. Such polarizing items are, after all, not only good for newspaper circulation, for listener and viewer ratings, but also for the levelling out of authority and any sense of values.

Given the way in which media 'balance' is often interpreted as the putting forward of two or more opposing views (whatever numbers, status or depth of learning stand behind each) both seem to be levelled out. So simple denunciations will be self-defeating, while church scandals will tell against the authority appealed to. Boeve's prescription for this case, and he is not alone, would point again to the kind of position possible for relative relativism.

It is precisely into the space created by the disavowal of grand narratives that the grand narrative of the market and the consumer has come. Boeve's 'economizational narrative' may take anything from medicines to ancient monuments defined as commodities within its scope. It would seem then that humans cannot do without *some* narrative to give identity and purpose in the world. Indeed, as Arran Gare has written:

> One of the consequences of the postmodern loss of faith in grand narratives, and all narratives to some extent, is to have revealed the importance of narratives for the constitution of subjects, social organizations and societies.[26]

Gare has environmentalism in mind, and the question why, when environmental consciousness has been raised worldwide, it has had so little effect in countering the economists' version of nature as raw material and commodities-in-waiting. The links between the ecological crisis, the globalization of capitalism and the disintegration of modern culture have not been knitted into a story that will move mountains:

> What is clearly lacking are stories of sufficient power and complexity to orient people for effective action to overcome environmental problems, to relate the multiplicity of social and cultural forms implicated in or affected by environmental destruction to reveal to people what roles they can play in this project.[27]

The story is thus necessary for the action, as it is with the churches, who also need to have revealed to them 'what roles they can play'. But, given the view that past grand narratives have been oppressive (concerning the domination of materialism, or Western culture and rationality, or ecclesiastical authority), what kind of narrative, implying what kind of stance, will do?

Boeve sees the current problem in terms of a unilateral claim to truth:

Both the relativistic pluralism of the market, as well as the authoritarian religious and fundamentalist counter-reaction pass over that which stands out in the post-modern crisis: that master narratives, which hegemonically claim the truth, forget that the truth is not something which can be possessed or controlled ... [N]arratives' attempt to include or control everything stumble at their boundaries because of stubborn resistances of irreducible residues of uncontrollableness.[28]

Gare argues that the new form of the stories does not have to be like the assured monologues of the past, which would incur Boeve's strictures. Instead there may be:

a second kind of narrative, a polyphonous, dialogical narrative in which a multiplicity of perspectives are represented, where through dialogue the narrative reflects on its own development.[29]

Such a narrative will have provisionality rather than the simple assertion of all-embracing truth. It will be what Boeve calls an *open* narrative, allowing that not everything may be controlled by it.

[T]hey will be narratives which seek to remain open for otherness, heterogeneity; that cannot be entirely appropriated ... Truth is not claimed but witnessed to, not possessed but loved ... Christian narratives, even if they are more than once tempted to claim absolute truth, are perhaps in their nature open narratives at best. As much as God lets Godself be known in history, God does not let Godself be enclosed in it.[30]

If Christians can renounce claims to an absoluteness of truth which is simply to be laid down for others they are in a much better position to comment on the absolutizing message of the market, and to dialogue with others rather than confront them with an exclusive master narrative. Relative relativism, then, allows the church to move on with belief in its own part of the dialogue which may attract others to share it, but will not be imposed as some kind of impossible, single, timeless truth.

# 4

# Withness

It is often illuminating to go back to a dictionary to find the full scope of even the simplest words. The Concise Oxford offers thirteen uses of 'with'. They are not all positive, as the verbs 'to fight with' and 'to break with' show. But even these have a background in engagement. More positively the definitions which have a bearing here are:

(a)  in or into company of, or relation to, among, beside;

(b)  agreeably or in harmonious relations to;

(c)  in same way or direction, or at the same time as.

From these definitions alone one may draw a picture of God with us. God is in our company, among us and beside us; not as a spy or a voyeur counting our sins, but agreeably, in a harmonious relationship (at least on the divine side). We are on the same way at the same time as God. We pilgrimage together.

There is a sense in which this is an inescapable relationship, since God relates to the whole of creation, human and non-human, Father-like. But there is also a sense in which we may *choose* this withness of God as friend and companion. These are unforced relations we enter at our own desire, and they turn the real though general 'with' of God into personal friendship and enlarging companionship. These are the effects of power working by attraction, permitting the other freedom to chose to enter the relationship.

But even as friends and companions of God, we remain the people we are. The preposition 'with' implies closeness and commonality of aim, but no take-over. God remains God, and we are who we are in our own context. Yet we remain humans with ongoing possibilities. We are not set in concrete and are open to influence and change from all kinds of sources, including our friends and companions. It is thus that God works in the world – not to interrupt or overturn the freedom of creation, but to encourage and persuade those open to the effects of divine presence in shaping how they should be and what they should do.

Such working between God and humans involves concurrence and synergy. Synergy is a word much favoured in business now as an intensive form of co-operation. It applies in business because it is efficient and energy-saving; it applies in theology because it is gracious and energy-giving. Literally it means the working together of energies, and the word coheres with the preference of Orthodox theologians for referring to divine energies rather than divine power. Thus Ion Bria, describing the interaction of gospel and culture in Romania, writes of a 'sense of epiphany, of the presence of uncreated divine energies in the empirical world'.[1] In that case 'grace is not something external and supernatural, but is intricately interwoven with God's creation'.

Even the Greek *dunamis* (power) is more dynamic in its connotations than the Latin *potentia* which has been the source of much Western thinking on God's power. And the Greek *energeia* is action, force, life, energy. In the synergy of 'with' that divine life and energy is offered to us to work alongside our finite efforts in thought and action in our own varied contexts. Concurrence likewise is literally 'running with', and one could say that concurrence is the spiritual alignment which occurs with God as Friend, while synergy is the joint use of energies abroad in the world. But the spiritual and the practical are not always so neatly divided. So our energies may run with God's, and our spiritual alignment may run humbly with the divine. Yet, because we are free, finite and fallible our energies may run in a much more self-concerned direction.

Power, in the sense of God's power and human power, was once thought of as a specified fixed amount, a quantum,

---

### The Flip Side of Synergy

***Why did the chicken cross the road?***

Andersen Consultants, in a partnering relationship with the client, helped the chicken by rethinking its physical distribution strategy and implementation processes ... Andersen Consultants convened a diverse cross-spectrum of road analysts and best chickens along with Andersen Consultants with deep skills in the transportation industry to engage in a two-day itinerary of meetings in order to leverage their personal knowledge capital, both tacit and explicit, and to enable them to synergize with each other in order to achieve the implicit goals of delivering and successfully implementing an enterprise-wide value framework across the continuum of poultry cross-median processes ...

*New Straits Times*, 5 April 1998

---

so that the more power was exercized by humans, the less could be attributed to God, and that appeared to infringe the omnipotence of the Godhead. At its peak in hypercalvinism, where logic elbowed out love, God's sovereignty was described as total, one hundred per cent of the quantum: all events, whether beneficial or injurious to humans, were entirely God's doing while humanity was entirely passive under divine rule. But since the Enlightenment humans have considered themselves much more in control, and on the quantum model God's power has seemed to shrink correspondingly, to the point of invisibility. But if power is thought of in terms of relations rather than in percentage of clout, the picture changes. On the synergy model God has always been, and remains, powerful and superior in the exercise of energies working along with what humans are capable of. Divine action and human action are not proportions of a quantum; instead each is fully its own in working together, though far from equal.

Further, to think in terms of synergy is to turn on its side and shake up the model of grace perfecting nature. That model, like that of a quantum of power, was applied onto-logically, that is, concerning the being of each person, which was conceived as human nature up to a point and beyond that perfected by supernatural grace. These two components have been 'conceived in such a way that they appear as two layers so carefully placed that they penetrate each other as little as possible'.[2] As that mention of 'layers' suggests, onto-logical conceptions of humanity tend to view human beings as some kind of containers into which grace is poured (infused). The following picture is something of a caricature, but with point. For Roman Catholics the part of the con-tainer holding nature was all right as far as it went (or could be restored to that position by confession and penance), although it always required perfecting by unknowable super-natural grace. For the Reformed the container was, so to speak, full of the holes of sin, so that it did not require completion so much as a bath of grace moment by moment. ('We have grace like beggars' – Calvin, Barth.) In a very neat expression of a very profound difference the Reformed-Roman Catholic dialogue comments:

> The Reformed insist more on the promise of a 'not-yet'; Catholics underline more the reality of gift 'already there'.[3]

But this ancient division of thought may be overcome. To move from an ontological to a relational model is to move the divine connection from the vertical to the horizontal axis, from the static container-filling to the dynamic interrelation-ship, and from God and humans considered separately to the two considered in relation. There remain conceptions of more and less, for God has infinitely more to contribute to the relationship. There is still nature in the sense of the kind of thought and action humans are capable of, and there is still sin, and grace. But sin, grace and nature are events rather than designations; they happen *ambulando* (en route) in a relationship rather than defining the connection once for all. And they are all mixed together in the ambiguity of circumstance, action and consequence. God's forgiveness does not so much restore nature to its 'proper' level, nor does it fall perpetually like rain on humans defined as sinners. Rather its necessity is the divine means of maintaining relationship and making its future possible. With God's presence in every part of the world and with every creature 'the whole life of man is constantly affected by grace'.[4]

The preposition 'with' has a different effect concerning God's relationship from the preposition 'in', though both are no more than means of expressing divine presence. If humans were indeed containers then 'in' would be the appropriate word for where God was to be found, and since I doubt the container model I also doubt this use of 'in'. Yet 'in' has a long and honourable tradition as the proper preposition for God's presence – *in* Christ, *in* men and women, *in* the church. God is thus seen to work from the inside, changing and directing people. I would not wish simply to depart from such usage, but it does have some difficulties. Where is human freedom if God is 'in' someone? If the freedom were still there, such that the person could go his or her own way, was God really 'in' that person even during the selfishness, or temporarily visiting until selfishness required divine departure?

On inspection the preposition is used when what I have called concurrence occurs, and God-imbued thought or action is perceived. It is never used of people going selfishly or viciously about the world. That would imply that God is absent from the person except for those times when God is 'in' his or her action. The same notion of absence becoming presence occurs in those hymns which call on God to come (*Veni, Creator Spiritus*). The conclusion appears to be that God's options are to be either absent or in, and that coheres with an understanding of God distant in transcendence who is to be called to come and inhabit the person or the church. (Paul's description of the Christian as 'in Christ' seems different – it is a constant state, a kind of benevolent micro-climate in which Christians always walk.)

If God is understood to have given creation freedom to develop and evolve, but also to have companioned it from the start, we do not need hymns calling on God to come, but rather hymns to open our eyes to God who is already there. Nor may we restrict our preposition for God's presence to one which connotes times when something visibly good is happening. At all times and in all circumstances God is *with* us whether or not we are open to concurrence with that presence. So God does not take us over, as 'in' might imply, and God's freedom is not encroached on either.

The church has appeared to have its importance as the place *in* which God is to be found. Thus the preposition 'in' gives it its importance, and the temptation to compare itself favourably with other places in which God is not. What, then, is its importance if God is always *with* us, both in and out of the church? The short answer is that the church is a focus, an enactment, a sharing and a meditation on what is always the case. The difference the church makes is not so much one of indwelt holiness in comparison with a secular world, as offering a concentrated perception of the holiness which is everywhere. There can be no division between sacred and secular when God is omnipresent. Further God's presence is always a creating/saving presence and in God's constancy cannot be out of character. So the church is not the home of a salvation which cannot be found outside it. That would arrogate too much power (power, not energy) to the church.

Yet for those who discover God's relationship as expressed through Christ the church fulfils an essential role. Here people may gather with others 'on the way'; the divine-human relationship is rehearsed formally (or often, now, less formally) in liturgy and sermon, while its origin is both portrayed and conveyed in Holy Communion, and its welcome in Baptism. I find the phrase 'Real Presence' unhelpful in modern speech, as if there could be degrees of reality in God's presence. What may happen instead is a concentrated perception of divine presence in church services when the concentration of the worshippers locks on to the always concentrated divine side of the relationship – concurrence and synergy in worship. Thus a church service both focusses and enacts in word and gesture the relationship which continues outside it in work and home and leisure.

But this is a relationship defined by 'with'. If what the church says and does does not embody this sense of withness, this sense of being alongside God and each other, encouraging each other on pilgrimage, what it does in its services will be only notional. Similarly, if a church is engaged in issues of peace and justice, but its services of worship glorify an exalted King, it speaks with double tongue. Coherence in what the church says and what the church does is greatly to be desired.

In so far as they have not yet changed, then, what the churches need to discover and put into practice in the midst of the plurality of postmodern Britain, is a way to express withness which is both attractive and effective. The second part of this book explores some possibilities. Because it refers to the church as a body, or group of bodies, in the world it is the church's companioning role which is described. Behind the possibility of that role, however, and giving it depth and durability, remain the realities of God as unconditionally loving parent and trustworthy friend.

The particularity of individual contexts also matter for this theology, but that cannot be described in this general account, so what is here is a vision of practice rather than a guidebook. Most chapters, moreover, are short although the topics are large; they are a spur to further thought and action in the reader's setting, not a prescription. That seemed to me potentially more attractive than exhaustive renderings which left no space for dialogue and application.

Finally, I realize that in the succeeding sections I have

described present possibilities in contrast to what went before, so that cumulatively that might appear as total criticism of the church of the recent past. But that was not my intention, however constrictive the past's lingering into the present may be, and however dubious from a contemporary perspective some of their practices were. People did what they saw to be right for their time. It is only as times have changed that what appeared right then may be so no longer, and the difference makes a good springboard for discussing the present – though here again, what seems eminently right and good now may well appear more dubious in the future. The relation to the past is best summed up in David Bosch's words:

> Humility also means showing respect for our forebears in the faith, for what they have handed down to us, even if we have reason to be acutely embarrassed by their racist, sexist and imperialist bias. The point is that we have no guarantee that we shall do any better than they did.[5]

# PART TWO

# Synergy in the Church

# 5

# Synergy involves Change

The change referred to in the title to this chapter is that from a church where the organization and values continue to mirror those of modernity, to one which is prepared to move on and experiment with postmodernity. That change is required, not out of a desire for fashionableness but because serious shortcomings have now, with a change of values, become visible in the modern paradigm and these will continue to hurt the church if they are continued. Adrian Hastings puts one side of the matter succinctly:

> In a time when human society is changing more rapidly than it has ever done before the church has to change, not just to keep up with the Joneses, but because it is the Joneses.[1]

The people in the church, especially the younger people still in the church, are among those being affected and changed by changes in society. If the church cannot address them in the midst of that change it will 'sink into being a sort of religious dimension of the National Trust' in Hasting's words. That is, it will be simply a collection of ancient monuments and heritage, the 'grave of God' indeed.

On the other hand there are some who come to church to escape the changes around, finding there an ark of security as the waters of change rise higher. Such people cannot simply be abandoned: a place must be found for them in a future, more diverse church. But if the preferences of those resisting change dictate the church's actions, that, writes Rahner, permits the church 'to go on in the old style until the very last bourgeois and rural oases of an historical epoch moving towards its end have more or less disappeared'.[2] We 'cannot be content to set our hopes on a little heap called the church, trusting to be delivered from the winds in history and society'.

---

'The General Assembly is the supreme court of the Church' is the gist of the Principal Clerk's response to John Chalmers' suggestions for the modernization of the assembly . . . That is, of course, the lawyer's answer. The Church of Scotland can draw so heavily today upon its constitution of hierarchical or nested courts because, historically, the church was developing constitutionally in parallel with the development of the secular courts of Scotland. But any constitutional system – be it by court, parliament, popular forum or despot – is necessarily a product of its time, and is subject to rise and decay with the changing ethos of the age and culture. In fact the court system of our Church . . . has lost touch with the temper of the age . . . The temper of our age demands within our Church something lighter, less beholden to judicial exactitude and traditional dignity; something more immediate, more responsive, more spontaneous – and it demands that at all its levels of management.

Quentin Blane, letter to *Life and Work*, November 1997

---

Juan Luis Segundo likewise inveighs against what he calls a 'Christendom mentality' enduring even today within the church. To discern its existence he asks a number of searching questions about people's conception of the faith, and how far that is dictated by their concern for security, including:

To what extent is unity and uniformity of expression valued above everything else, while those who do not express this in traditional terms are criticized severely? To what extent does the Christian want Christians to be protected from any or all non-Christian ideologies that might jeopardize their own certitudes?[3]

These quotations are all from Roman Catholics, but the same suspicion of change at large, and the same desire for the security of continuity of things as they are affects all churches. I am certainly aware of their existence in the Church of Scotland. The Roman Catholic Church had the benefit of Vatican II with its Constitution on the Church to concentrate and give direction to the mind on this matter, while other churches have come much more piecemeal to similar conclusions.

The same breadth of application to all churches may be seen in the Roman Catholic Vincent Donovan's acute strictures on the character of the church at present.[4] These spell out in greater detail the increasingly deleterious effects of what Will Storrar called the marriage of the church to modernity with its ways and values. I will be commenting on these from time to time in relation to the church I know best, the Church of Scotland. But I hope that readers will also make their particular applications to their home churches. Donovan has four areas of complaint.

First, the church has moved from desiring unity to imposing uniformity both at home and in mission overseas where only one Western form of liturgy, sacraments and theology was admissable. The result of this implicit claim that 'there is only one way to do things and that is our way' has been observed also by David Bosch:

Catholicism endorsed the principle that a 'missionary church' must reflect in every detail the Roman custom of the moment. Protestants were scarcely more progressive in this regard ... [T]he churches on the mission field were structured on exactly the same lines as those on the missionaries' home front, where a completely different socio-economic system obtained.[5]

In time this came to mean that churches, having achieved uniformity at home, were more given to duplicating themselves abroad than to the original missionary impulse. What Scherer writes about Lutheran missions applies equally to other churches and the results may still be seen in European pride over a world-wide 'church family'.

> The Kingdom of God was reduced to a strategy by which Lutheran mission agencies planted Lutheran churches around the world. Questions were seldom asked at this time about the relationship of these churches to the Kingdom of God. Their very existence appeared to be its own justification, and no further discussion of mission goals was required.[6]

The point of dwelling on what happened on the mission field is that it was an extension of what had already happened at home in Britain, until occasional developments in the very recent past. The same structures, liturgical shapes and denominationally appropriate activities were expected in every congregation in every context, rich or poor, rural or urban. Against all that drive to uniformity Donovan argues for diversity in the proclamation of and response to the Christian message, and even more freedom in the 'liturgical, ministerial, sacramental and organizational carrying out of that message'.[7] The issue is not whether diversity may happen here and there quietly in the corners of some church, but whether the church at large affirms publicly that its nature is to be diverse, in its diverse contexts, while still being the church.

Donovan's next criticism is also quite applicable outside the Roman Catholic church, although there will be individual variations. He complains that the church has moved from generalization to specialization, such that certain people have become experts in, for instance, theology or spirituality, and these are no longer seen as something for everyone to be involved in creatively. As someone who is paid to study, think, write and teach theology I suppose I have a vested interest in this question. But it seems to me less a matter of whether there are specialists, as whether these specialists help others on, or whether all others are disempowered by the specialists' dominion. A theologian who provokes others into thinking theologically, as opposed to one who simply tells others 'this is how it is', is doing her/his job in a way that escapes this criticism. A practitioner in spirituality who encourages others into spiritual exploration is equally exempt.

The issue Donovan is attacking is the concentration of power in the church in the hands of 'experts' who in a top-down manner simply hand out what is to be believed and done to the rest. And although contra-indications may be advanced, such as the way the General Assembly of the Church of Scotland has frequently rejected what is proposed to it by its own Panel on Doctrine, all churches to some extent, and particularly the laity, suffer from, and are silenced by, the manner of experts.

The third criticism Donovan makes is universal among churches: the move to centralization, with control exercised from a central powerhouse. The fear is that if control is removed chaos will result. There may be ways of exercising central control other than through the bishops of this quotation, but the result is the same.

> The drive for centralization was so intense that bishops could not be happy with different departments, such as liturgy or social works or youth ministry or Catholic education scattered over the diocese. They could not be satisfied until all the heads of the departments of the diocese were gathered together under the bishop's wing in a single chancery building under one roof – preferably a skyscraper, a tower of power – in the heart of a city. Then every decision of any importance would pass through the bishop's office in a smoothly running display of the machinery of church government. No automobile factory could run more efficiently.[8]

The answer to this personal centralization is not necessarily to have central committees. Great dissatisfaction with them has been voiced in the Church of Scotland also:

> Assembly Boards and Committees are too little serving the congregations and too much serving the central church's agenda. The material with which Boards and Committees bombard Presbyteries and congregations is not always seen as user-friendly, does not always take adequate account of the average congregation . . .[9]

All such totalizing centralization militates against diversity, against doing what is needed or is most productive locally, and against the belief that the grace of God may be found and given visible form without reams of directives from central church offices bringing everyone into line. Some organization is undoubtedly necessary, but issues of how much, and of what kind, I shall leave to the last chapter.

To these modernist faults Donovan adds concentration:

> Concentration of many people in one place of worship is more efficient. It serves more people. But it pulls people out of their natural neighbourhoods in which they are going to have to live out their Christianity, and it gathers them in such density that there is no hope of ever finding in its midst the experience of community.[10]

Concentration in the Church of Scotland, in the shape of the Union and Readjustment Committee, now more smoothly, but no less powerfully, called Parish Reappraisal, was propelled, not by questions of how the gospel was to be preached in every corner of the country, but by whether parishes could afford an ordained minister, and whether there were enough of the ordained to go round. Nothing less than an ordained Minister of Word and Sacrament would do, while auxiliary (non-stipendiary) ministry appeared to be no better than an occasional stop-gap (even the name is condescending). Lay ministry, to the best of my knowledge, was scarcely considered. There was no thought that this financial exigency was exactly the moment to train and empower local lay leadership.

On the one hand this concentration on the ordained ministry implied an exclusive doctrine of ministry which had never been spelled out within the church. On the other, that enforced concentration on unions and readjustments of parishes probably caused more local heartache than any other action of the Kirk – heartache which was never given any value in relation to the lack of income. Further, whereas Donovan speaks of a resulting 'density', the Church of Scotland's experience is different. People were not prepared to be 'pulled out of their natural neighbourhoods' and preferred to leave the church, so that the united church often finished with the same number of members as *one* of the uniting congregations had previously.

Finally Donovan discussed maximization, the primacy of size and numbers. Again all churches may see their concerns reflected.

> Numbers of communicants and penitents and marriages determined the vitality of a parish. The amount of money taken in Sunday collections spoke of the status of a parish. Counting all these things and writing them down was of paramount importance in the welter of business-like administration, accountant mentality and book-keeping by double entry that became the job-description of a successful pastor – working his way up to a *bigger* parish.[11]

In many churches even local accounting is left to accountants, but numbers and statistics are still held to matter everywhere. Numbers are precisely what Storrar believes will lose their importance in postmodernity. But as things are at the moment, it would be a pity if any church distanced itself from these accusations because they are made from the context of Roman Catholicism in a book by a Church of

Scotland minister. What is at issue here is beyond denomi-nationalism in Britain. Indeed, from Donovan's survey the surprising thing is how much character in common the various churches of the West have, from the Baptists to the Roman Catholics, however different their theologies and other practices. The cultural forces have been inescapable, and from a different viewpoint may be seen to have negative spin-offs as well as the positive valuations which brought them about.

In none of the church relations described by Donovan is there any room for those defined by 'with'. The appropriate preposition would be 'over' – the centre over the periphery, numbers over spiritual effectiveness, experts over laity, uni-formity over local difference. This is not simply a matter of church preferences, but rather of power being used to impose, not to attract. Perhaps in days when authority was less questioned attraction was not seen to be necessary. But clearly, if 'God with us' is to be central to the church's thinking, much will have to change.

Change, however, is always a risk, and there are certainly risks in moving away from the church or modernity in which everyone at present has grown up and to which they are accustomed. For the move, to turn Donovan's criticisms on their head, will be to something much less tightly organized, considerably less powerful in the top-down sense, less uni-form and more diverse, and quite unpreoccupied with num-bers. All of that will be risky, but unless all the church's energies, money, organization and prayers are going to be directed to the preservation of what Rahner called 'this little heap', it is clear that change must come soon. Indeed it must come in the form of what Konrad Raiser has called 'the painful process of deinstitutionalizing',[12] a process of launch-ing into the future without the support of presently known structures, but with a vision of a different way of doing things.

Edward Patey, envisaging the same process for the Church of England, finds confidence in the risk God took in the

Incarnation, and indeed in all divine relations with human beings.

> [T]he God of the Bible is not a play-safe God. At every point he reveals himself as a risk-taker. Nor is his church called to play safe. It is to be a movement of men and women committed to explore the yet undiscovered purpose of God for his people who have their eyes fixed on the unknown future.[13]

God takes the risk of being friend and companion to women and men, and will companion the church through its changes to a more companionable form.

There are bound to be mistakes as we dismantle and experiment. And if companionship is the key not even those who are most wedded to things as they are may be abandoned. They and their churches may become part of the diversity in our pluralist society. The move is from what Karl Barth once called a 'hope and a yearning'[14] concerning the visible church to an implementation of patterns which will enact that hope as well as humans can – enact in the senses both of putting it into action, and of portraying it for others to see.

In much current understanding there is a readiness for change and in places experiments have begun. To give an instance of theological change: although power and dominion are still being exercised in our world, as they were when the church organized itself vertically, with at least a power divide between clergy and laity, these are no longer seen as images of power to copy in our churches. I sometimes ask first-year students, working in groups, to come up with images of God from contemporary society. They never suggest General, or Managing Director, or President. When I ask why not, they are horrified at the oppressive power relations involved. They do not have the same difficulty with King or Judge, mostly because these are traditional and largely honorific titles, but partly because they have never seen royal or judicial power actually exercised. They find it really difficult to come up with suitable images of God from today, which says something about both current society and changes in the perception of God. But one class voted overwhelmingly for God as a 'lollipop man', who goes with people into the traffic and sees them safely across. That would certainly be one model of 'God with us'.

Further to the notion that change is already happening, there are experiments going on everywhere: in worship styles, often with much increased congregational participation; in collaborative ministry; in ecumenical endeavours and interfaith encounters. I shall be elaborating on these in what follows. But the process is not clear cut. It may well be for a time what Hastings called

a muddled process in a muddled church. So it was and so it still will be, if we are going to adhere to a model . . . of a pilgrim church whose rules are never quite laid down in advance.[15]

What is needed now is that such individual efforts, which both point the way to the future with the theology and practice they imply, and protest at the present state of the church, become the churches' 'up front' acknowledged account of their change of being in contemporary society. Then they may be thoroughly evaluated and persuasively encouraged rather than being permitted here and there without acknowledgment, and in ways which do not seriously challenge the status quo. For in Moltmann's pregnant words:

Through its order, its ministries and its organization the church either confesses or denies the thing it has to represent.[16]

# 6

# Community and its Ministry

The burden of this chapter may be summed up in saying that the working out within the local church of relationships defined by 'with' will, at its best, produce fellowship and a sense of community. Ministry in that case is what lives with, companions, encourages and energizes that community. Thus ministry is not here defined at large as a calling or a role in relation to 'the church' as an abstract or even a theological entity, but rather in relation to the particularly of God-with, real and effective to a community. Ministry, then, may be more like that in the earliest Christian communities, before an overarching structure took place. But unlike these communities there is now the possibility of networking, interaction and joint effort. This is not the granular individualism of separate communities, but a church where power, such as in relevant decision-making, has been devolved to localities and to local members who have to face their own responsibilities and opportunities for using the power to attract.

Community, however, is one of the most overused words of our time. It has joined motherhood and apple pie as something no one can object to, yet it is almost emptied of particular meaning. Once, when the inhabitants of a housing estate were referred to as a community that may have been from a wish to bestow an air of cohesion and co-operation on the place – which was not necessarily there. Now the reference is simply to the people of a geographical location. Yet 'community' can be redeemed from bland collectivity.

Community is an aerosol word, popularly sprayed into discussions, giving a sweet scent and a hint of mist, clouding analysis. It is notorious that there is a mass of competing definitions. But all exist within the general framework of a discussion of personal relationships between human beings in groups, in society, and in the total 'human community'.[1]

And, since we have no other word for it, and since it is related to communion, with all its religious overtones, the word may be used to express a group sense of being with others and with God in church.

Jean Vanier of l'Arche Community has given much thought to what community may mean, not only for the disabled, but in general. First, to be in communion, to be in community:

> means to *be with* someone and discover that we actually belong together, communion means accepting people just as they are, with all their limits and inner pain, but also with their gifts and their beauty and their capacity to grow.[2]

When that is related to the church it is clearly not an easy first step, and impossible if people do not know each other, and are given, or take for themselves, no opportunity to meet and talk and discover each other. There will, of course, be people who are difficult, or so different that 'being with' is a problem. Vanier himself once said that a community is the place where the person you least want to live with always lives. But a l'Arche Community is full-time, day and night, while church communities are less demanding, if still requiring effort.

The effort is made easier for churches, perhaps, by Vanier's second point:

> To be in communion with someone also means to *walk with* them . . . for a mother who has just lost her child, or

for a woman who has just been abandoned by her husband
there is no answer, there is just the pain. What they need is
a friend who is willing to walk with them in all that pain.[3]

Vanier's words are certainly true of the sensitivity required
for those members of a church community who have recent,
or long-buried, pain. But there is another sense of 'walking
with' for churches – doing things together, whether that is
planning a service or feeding the homeless or whatever. It is
often in shared activities, even shared difficulties that the 'togetherness' of community is fostered. Thus churches where
congregations do little or nothing towards the way things go
have not begun 'walking with' towards community.

> God, you often take us by surprise;
> you do not tell us your name.
> You make yourself known to us
> in the events that happen along the way.
>
> God, give us the courage to take risks
> to build a highway in the desert
> when we do not see
> how we can possibly move forward.
> Give us courage to believe that you are here
> and will be ahead of us when we dare to move.
>
> Give us courage to believe that we as a church
> will find you there,
> to honour the things we dare to do,
> when we are prepared to take the risk
> and carry the first rock to build the highway.
>
> *Spirit, Gospel, Cultures,*
> WCC Publications 1995, p.31

Vanier's third point simply stands on its own as a reminder for all versions of community:

> But this communion is not fusion. Fusion leads to *confusion*. In a relationship of communion you are you and I am I. I have my identity and you have yours. I must be myself and you must be yourself. We are called to grow together, each one becoming more fully himself or herself. communion . . . is not possessiveness.[4]

For churches the impulse towards, and the goal of, all the effort is the understanding of community with God who is with us, walks with us, but allows us to be ourselves. Church community is the imperfect, finite but real endeavour to live out that relationship with others. Thus, in the words of Vatican II's Pastoral Constitution on the Church in the Modern World (*Gaudium et spes*):

> The Church, at once a visible assembly and a spiritual community, goes forward together with humanity and experiences the same earthly lot which the world does. She serves as a leaven and a kind of soul for human society.[5]

Yet there may be such practical difficulties and opportunities for division in any local church working towards community that the endeavour could make the last state of that church worse than the first. Robin Greenwood, once 'a parish priest with some pretensions to working out a vision for myself and others' discovered the difficulty of 'expecting everyone to fit into . . . carefully constructed theories about the church'.[6]

It is so easy for clergy, who put so much time and emotional effort into the institutional church for so many reasons, to convince ourselves that the church is a community, when it is actually nothing of the sort.[7]

The warning is salutary. A vision imposed is simply another instance of top-down power from the clergy. And no church may simply be told that they are to be a community. Karl Popper has some wise words on the dangers of a misplaced zealousness far more demanding than Greenwood's in the implementing of ideals:

> Of all political ideals, that of making the people happy is perhaps the most dangerous one. It leads invariably to the attempt to impose our scale of 'higher' values upon others in order to make them realize what seems to us of greatest importance for their happiness; in order, as it were, to save their souls . . . We all feel certain that everybody would be happy in the perfect community of our dreams. And, no doubt, there would be heaven on earth if we could all love one another. But . . . the attempt to make heaven on earth invariably produces hell. It leads to intolerance. It leads to religious wars, and to the saving of souls through the Inquisition.[8]

There may, therefore, be no imposition of solutions, including my own efforts, with the intolerant implication that those who do not wish to join are somehow recalcitrant or out of touch. Indeed the proposal I am about to make has a place for those who do not wish to change. But there are plenty who do, who find the current regular diet of worship and church life unsustaining; or who simply stay away; or who have never been attracted to it. Many local churches, in some effort to meet their (in fact) diverse constituencies, have more than one kind of service, one traditional, the other, say, a livelier version for young people. The question then is whether this results in *two* communities in the one church which rarely interact. There is also the matter of who ministers to both, and how.

What the model of diverse services implies is 'horses for courses', the kind of worship and involvement suitable for identifiable groups within the church. It seems to me that

that model of diversity could be taken further into the conception of different churches or communities intended for different groups. To some extent that is happening already. The Scottish Episcopal Church, for instance, although it is small in Scotland as a whole, has enough churches in Edinburgh to provide every version of episcopal worship, from 'bells and smells' to 'happy clappy', from a musically-endowed cathedral to low-church evangelical worship, and most versions in between. Episcopalians in Edinburgh may join the church which most attracts them (so, of course may Presbyterians, but their range of offered options tends to be narrower). I presume that each Episcopalian congregation does network with others and has responsibilities beyond its own members, so this is an example of interlinked communities. In this example, of course, I have left out the roles of the Bishop, the Dean and all central authority in order to concentrate on the possibility of diverse communities.

The diversity in any church already exists – as Hastings said, 'We are the Joneses.' There are those for whom spirituality – environmental, Celtic, Eastern – is the most effective way to God. There are also those who are uplifted by charismatic engagement. Some want to see the church more involved in local or national issues of peace and justice, while others prefer the more sedate status quo, or are moved by the music of Bach and Palestrina, or the language of the liturgy. At the moment such diversity is not, for the most part, officially recognized or encouraged. But given the desirability of community, and given also the human difficulty in bringing it about, it would be possible for churches actively to encourage clusters of diverse communities in cities and rural towns with satellite villages. This would also be an excellent opportunity for working ecumenically.

This solution may seem like an evasion from facing up to the difficulties of community in churches as they are, but on the one hand difficulties in the shape of difficult people will still be around, and on the other, diversifying may help the church to go forward rather than stalling. Interaction between communities would also always be possible. But to make local variety acknowledged policy, especially with local decision-making, may seem dangerous to those who wish a uniform church over which there may be control, and indeed the dangers exist. Experiments may go wrong, or key people may be missing or inadequate. But these are simply different dangers from those the church faces at present while it dwindles. It would not be a move from present security to potential danger.

The change would have to be made attractive to, and owned by, the church at large – more easily written than achieved – for it would lose the character of companionship if most were unwilling. It would require some initial organization, best done in a local district, and some local oversight which did not lose the sense of being with the worshippers. Budgets would have to be allocated. But the tight structuring and the centralization which at present defines the church's activities would have gone.

Each community in a cluster is likely to be small (a 'human' size, where people may know each other) and mostly postmodern in style. Each may well have a web-site to make communication with others easy and enlarging. Members, or, rather, attenders, may well come and go in postmodern fashion, as they are attracted and as their religious needs change. Someone, for instance, who starts with a participative and highly visual, active service may well move on to something more traditional when their job demands exhaust them, and what they want on Sunday is to receive.

So a church which takes on board both the call to fellowship and the criticisms encapsulated by Donovan will plan for a dismantling of its present bureaucracy and centralized committee structure, will enable and encourage diverse groups to form for worship and work as part of that church's diversity. It will concentrate on power as attraction rather than force, just as God attracts rather than overwhelming, and enjoys diversity. None of that will be easy: it would be easier simply to let the present church decay. But that is to

---

### For English read British?

The study of reconciliation as a task for the church, using case studies from real life, would not be complete without taking into account cultural values and norms which are peculiarly English. No theological reflection today can ignore the central place of culture without being guilty of extreme naivety. Thus, in this case, a Christian community would have to come to grips with the almost unqualified distaste that the English have for 'extreme' solutions . . . and their desire to find, where possible, moderate, compromising (understand 'sensible') ways forward. In the light of the biblical revelation of God in Jesus Christ, is this cultural characteristic a correct intuition of a genuine path to the healing of relationships, or is it a papering-over of deep-seated discriminations which always has the effect of leaving the ruling classes in the ascendancy?

Andrew Kirk, 'Liberal Theology and Local Theologians' in *Theology in the City* ed A. Harvey, SPCK 1989, p.29

---

turn the church into a ghetto, a laager for the remains of the faithful, a shrinking and wizened Body of Christ. And that is not what God calls us to.

But who will take responsibility and lead these communities? Even the most communal and democratic will need, at least sometimes, someone at whom the buck stops, someone who ensures continuity, and someone who sees that worship is worship of God and not simply the self-indulgence of the like-minded. That could be a lay person with the appropriate gifts, energy, time and training, chosen by the community and recognized by the church at large, but even that would not mean there was no role for the ordained as at present. It may simply mean that ministry itself becomes more diverse. Certainly in the short term priests and ministers who are convinced of the primacy of 'with' will be needed as church members find their way in new circumstances.

The most priestly thing an ordained person does (apart from ordering the sacrament, a matter to which I shall return) is to represent the people to God and God to the people. That remains. But how it is effected depends very much on the understanding of God involved. When God was thought of primarily as the distant sovereign, the minister/priest was, so to speak, the channel of communication, or the channel of learning; thus the one who, in the sacraments, oversaw the making tangible of the mystery of God; the one who prayed to God on behalf of the people, and addressed the people on behalf of God. Calvin's words, which will come as a surprise to those who think the Reformed have a low view of ministry, is that the minister is 'to represent his (God's) person'.[9]

But if the God whose person is to be represented is God-with, God alongside all people, sharing our experiences, encouraging synergy and concurrence with the divine energies, then ordained ministry itself takes on a different aspect. Prayer for the people of the church continues, a communing with God over all that goes on in the community. What may also continue is ensuring that the word of God, in whatever medium it is expressed, is faithfully portrayed and attended to. But if God is with everyone, the sole channel image of priesthood is superseded by an image of many channels in lively use within the community, and if the minister is still to represent God to the people that will be by being with them as God is with them, encouraging divine-human and human-human synergy and concurrence, sometimes challenging or restraining, but without breaking companionship.

Within that understanding of God there is a leadership role as churches change. Perhaps 'encouraging change' should become part of theological education, for change cannot simply be imposed if it is to succeed. And indeed no change will be possible in the church if ministers in large numbers decide that present arrangements with their present position are preferable. Greenwood, in his Leeds parish, did effect a shift such that 'the laity of the parish have been encouraged to share in ministry and the whole ethos is one of collegiality rather than hierarchy'.[10]

One instance of his changes concerned priest and people in eucharist worship. It 'is not a ritualistic action beautifully presented by a handful of people in a separate room within the church [the sanctuary], on behalf of the majority of passive onlookers, also in their own room [the nave]'.[11] (In passing I would wish to say that within the hoped-for future diversity there will still be a place for aesthetically enriching ritual for onlookers who may be no more passive than those watching a play or studying a work of art.) For very many churches what Greenwood writes would hold true:

> Our theology is that we are sharing in a communion meal with Christ our Lord at the centre. *All* of us are celebrating with equal responsibility, though the clergy will be holding it all together.[12]

If that is the theology, the practice should make it able to be experienced by all. So Greenwood shifted the altar/communion table into the nave, the room which all shared. Similarly, from a different tradition, my home church reverts regularly to the old Scottish custom of setting a long table down the nave (possible again thanks to moveable chairs) round which communicants stand, about forty at a time, serving each other with the bread and wine at the distribution of the elements. Communion is then physically central, it is shared and the minister remains the one appointed by God and the church to enable it to happen.

The question whether *only* the minister/priest may 'hold it all together' at Holy Communion in Greenwood's words is currently under discussion. Moltmann for one sees all ministry as arising from and elected by the local congregation:

[Christ's] invitation involves no condition about the acknowledgment of ministries in the church. It is gracious, unconditional and prevenient like the love of God itself. Everyone whom he calls and who follows his call has the authority to break the bread and dispense the wine. The administration of the supper is the 'ministry' of the whole congregation and every person who is called. The acknowledgment of a 'special' ministry obscures Christ's giving of himself 'for all' and the fellowship of brothers and sisters which all are to enter.[13]

Whether or not Moltmann's vision of what he calls 'the Messianic fellowship' comes about finally it cannot seriously be adopted from where the churches now are. If ministers do work in a spirit of collegiality rather than hierarchy; if God is with each manifestation of the church where it is with its present members; and if these members have the time, the calling and the assistance to serve as ordained ministers do now, things may change.

From a Roman Catholic point of view Adrian Hastings already finds the clergy-laity divide unclear, especially with the decline in numbers of clergy.

Yet it may well be that the decline of the clergy is the *sine qua non* for the rebirth of the phoenix. The more the church hangs on to a mediaeval concept of clergy the more it must decay, the more it recognizes the theological groundlessness and modern social irrelevance of the clergy/laity distinction, the more it may live. Probably the church really will be a matter of basic communities – worshipping and thinking groups far smaller and more intimate than most present parishes, meeting less formally, sharing ideas more deliberately.[14]

Moltmann and Hastings are unlikely bed-fellows, and if the future of the church looks rather similar to both of them that must be taken with full seriousness. The Church of England has already gone some way down that road.

> Instead of blandly praying for more ministers as the church had bidden us to do, we were beginning to ask whether the short supply of clergy was part of a divine strategy to shake the church out of a complacency lulled by long-standing accepted ways of running the ecclesiatical machine.[15]

Patey rehearses the advantages of a locally-ordained ministry arising from the report *Faith in the City*:

> it creates a fully local church, deriving its identity from the people in a particular place working out the way of living faithfully to the gospel by taking full account of the local culture. It reconciles the local church to the local community, encouraging a close identity between the two. It can be seen as part of the recognition by the church that traditional ways alone will not enable it to meet its responsibility to local Christian communities in such areas.[16]

Even if locally ordained, or freely elected lay members of a community became the way of the church in the future, there is certainly a role for the ordained ministry of today, with and not over the heads of members, to bring about change.

A church where members are 'with' each other will have liturgy, or part of it, arising from the members' situation. As Ann Morisy, a Church of England Community Ministry Adviser expresses it: 'Liturgy, if it is to be described as 'apt', needs to express people's deepest fears and hopes.'[17] But further it puts these fears and hopes into the context of the Christian faith. In small groups people may make their own liturgies, discovering in the process that 'liturgy is one of the most profound, as well as the most convivial, activities known to humankind'. Likewise Nicholas Bradbury in the inner city finds a clear need:

'to connect worship and ordinary feeling, and for liturgy to transcend the communication gap between different styles of language, barriers of social class and educational background.[18]

Meeting a lay reader at a Diocesan Synod I asked how things were going. In tears, she described how a new incumbent had decided that preaching and teaching were his gift. After years of valued and full ministry of leading groups and preaching she had been 'stood down' . . . A few days later a vicar rang up incensed because a lay member of his congregation had been invited to help with some diocesan training and the request had not been channelled through him to determine what his lay people should or should not be invited to consider. Shortly after-wards a clergyman who has seen himself as being facilita-tive and encouraging of lay ministry was brought up short as he became aware of how constantly he talked about 'my parish', 'my people', 'my patch', as though somehow he owned them . . . 'His' lay people are fortunate that he chooses to share 'his' ministry with them – many clergy don't. Another colleague describes this as the 'grace and favour' nature of shared ministry.

Chris Peck, Director of Laity
Development for Liverpool Anglican diocese,
'Deluded Servants', *Christian*, 96/2

One might say equally that it has to transcend the communi-cation gap with today's young, which includes moving from the verbal to the visual, as well as including local people in crafting particular locally relevant liturgies. Hastings would agree, yet with a valuable reservation:

A workable liturgy needs emphatically to be participat-able now, it requires then a living relationship with

contemporary culture and consciousness, but its relationship to the culture of the present is a rather different one
– or should be – from, say, a pop song: its function as a
vehicle of meaning, a *memoriale* of all that mattered most
in the past, and a gateway to the transcendent, really
requires that its relationship to contemporary culture be
not too close a fit.[19]

Ann Morisy, however, with her emphasis on empowering
local liturgy, points to a tension which may well become
common if a real movement for change is mooted in the
churches. What at the moment brings renown or kudos in
the church – nurturing small local Christian cells or setting
up an organization with a high profile?

The irony is that reputations in the church, and in society
as a whole, are not made through sustaining a modest,
volunteer-run community project. Enviable reputations are
more likely to be achieved by building up a formidable
voluntary organization which has an array of strategies
for addressing the needs of its client group. In committing
themselves to a community ministry approach, church
leaders have to be alert to the tension within the model,
and the possible tension within themselves. Community
ministry requires people to achieve sufficient control over
their ego needs to appreciate that the reward is in heaven
or not at all.[20]

After generations of 'thinking big', of responding to a
situation by setting up a committee or other structure within
the church with a solution to be applied universally, the move
away from Donovan's criticized centralization and concentration will involve 'thinking small', thinking local, thinking
in the here and now in which God is with us; networking
in give and take with other localities rather than designing
overall strategies.

Implicit in what has just been written is the view that if

the church of the future is to be composed of clusters of smaller communities, there may be much to learn from community ministry in the church as it is at present, even though future communities may be much more diverse socially and economically. Skills in support and advocacy may be needed everywhere. David Thomas, for instance, perceives a need for ministry to be something much more submerged than the kind of leadership which is solo and out in front, even if that is perceived to be on behalf of others:

Community work is the enabling or empowering process of face-to-face work, *with* rather than *for* groups of local people who have identified their needs and wish to work collectively to do something about it. If it is about enabling people to do things for themselves, then in today's urban areas that is not only a crucial intervention, but one that is complex, demanding and requiring the highest standards in skills and personal qualities.[21]

Much of the church's social work has been thought of as giving a helping hand, or a voice to the voiceless. There may still be occasions when that is genuinely needed. But it tends to the power structure of the one who has the power speaking *for* the powerless, which may leave them as beneficiaries, but still basically powerless, and clients. Now the perception is that the powerless are to discover their own power with unobtrusive support. In one of the few reflective statements in their excellently practical book *Mission Statements*, the Association of Scottish Community Ministers writes:

The skills needed in this kind of situation are to be an enabler who works in a supportive and encouraging manner to coach and build up people's fragile confidence. The worker who adopts this ethos of working is exposed to constant analysis, of self and of others, never shrinking from doubt and dedicated to truth. This ensures that people themselves do not become dependent on the worker, but instead become capable and able to do the work themselves. Thus the style of work is such that those active in it are continually working themselves out of one situation and into another.[22]

---

### The Issue of Physical Disabilities

[Any church needs] to look at its own community. Is it an environment that is open to persons with disabilities? This concerns the physical facilities: for instance, are they accessible to people who need wheelchairs, or can people with hearing disabilities take part in the activities of the churches? It is also a challenge to the attitude towards persons with disabilities within the churches. Do we see them as a weak group that need to be taken care of, or do we recognize that persons with disabilities have a ministry within the churches? It is important to understand that it is not a question simply about how the churches should help people with disabilities, but what persons with disabilities can give to the churches.

Interim Statement on the theology and empirical understanding of the issue of disabilities, Lay Participation towards Inclusive Community Working Group, WCC 1997

---

The Board of Social Responsibility of the Church of England have grappled with this issue too, as part of its response to *Faith in the City*. It began with theology and a set of values to underpin the work. Here, first, are the values which are cited because they apply not only in relation to the church's work in deprived areas, but as those which may express themselves in the future church for all:

(a) A vision of a co-operative society in which people live together peacefully and control the environment in which they live.

(b)  A perspective on humanity that gives equal value to all people whatever their condition . . .

(c)  A view of equality and justice that acknowledges the right of all people to have equal chances of meeting human needs . . .

(d)  A commitment to sharing power and responsibility with people in the community

(e)  A recognition that genuine participation and collaborative styles of work are to the benefit of all who are involved and are the most creative ways of solving problems.[23]

If churches may agree that these are the kinds of values suitable for the inner city, it is difficult to see why they are not suitable for their own organization and practices at large.

The theology of the Board of Social Responsibility describes a vision of interdependence and interrelatedness in the Kingdom of God, invoking the practice of Jesus in taking people's life-experiences seriously together with the struggles for justice and righteousness in many biblical stories.

God calls men and women to change systems and structures that diminish people and leave them powerless.[24]

Presumably that is true also of systems and structures in the church everywhere.

It is interesting to see that the almost universal reference to empowerment is in complete contrast to much recent theology, especially since Moltmann's *The Crucified God*, which has been concerned with God's vulnerability, fellow suffering and the power of powerlessness to attract and change people.[25] That may well have been the response of a Western Christianity which found itself marginalized and powerless in society. Some undoubtedly found this an effective depiction, but it did nothing for the situation of the actually powerless in society. Perhaps in Britain now there is more hope of change, at least here and there, than complete powerlessness would allow. The vision of God in this book is

not of one who is powerless, nor a liberator, exactly, in the
Latin American style. In some ways the God whom I have
described has a power like yeast, making changes possible
when synergies occur. These changes in the understanding of
God fit neatly into a Hegelian triad. First there is the thesis of
the omnipotent sovereign God; then the antithesis of the
powerless crucified God; finally (for the moment) the synthesis of a God who is powerful, but powerful to attract and
empower rather than to rule. Ministry now is in the service
of that God, whoever performs it.

Thus far I have been writing for the most part as if one
person still led a church community. But that is far from
being the only possibility. Even now it has become common
enough in England and Wales, though hardly known north
of the border, to have various forms of collaborative ministry. Sometimes, at present, the collaboration is among a
group of the ordained, and sometimes ministers with lay
people in a congregational team. This is clearly an extension
of the principle of withness, but its introduction requires
nurturing rather than the fiat of some denomination or local
minister; indeed what is needed is what Malcolm Grundy
once called a 'gradual, mutual evolution'.

The problems with this, as with all versions of change,
ought not to be minimized, even if they are not finally deci-
sive. There have been occasions when collaborative ministry
has not worked, as Keith Pound notes regarding ministers,
the group with which I shall begin, turning to the laity later.

Everything is not lovely in the collaborative ministry
garden. There are areas of such ministry which fail. Formal
teams of full-time ministers which come together have been
known to split up again with much hurt and bruising, and
where this has happened the last state of those involved is
worse than the first. The strain of being expected to work
in new ways with inadequate resources can lead to much
unhappiness, to tensions which are far from creative, and
even to the breakdown of the team or group.[26]

Pound suggests that the cause of this unhappiness is in part a lack of training for the new situation into which people are placed, although undoubtedly there are some people who are temperamentally unsuited to working in teams. (In a diverse church with traditional as well as changing congregations there may be room for these as well.) But in comparison with the lengths to which businesses are prepared to go to train people to work in teams the church's approach may seem very naive and trusting. Selection assessments for big business include a team skills component, and a similar aspect to churches' selection schools could be more important than it currently is. Serving ministers would need retraining for collaboration. That should be no hardship or insult. Most people have to retrain today as change accelerates.

There is also an implication for theological education here, for teaching is most often done by an individual directed to a collection of individuals, with little encouragement towards shared work or projects. It is very hard to expect those who have had no experience suddenly to become a useful, but not dominant, part of a team. Teamwork is, however, one of the 'transferable skills' tertiary education is now required to provide. Further, students are often slow to connect theology with practice, and such team work can be presented as embodying God with us, showing both the possibilities and the difficulties of synergy and concurrence while the style of relationship would be learned practically.

Dennis Gardner writes out of long experience of collaborative ministry and its recommendation, both to the Methodist Church and to the old British Council of Churches. He spells out its implications:

For ordained ministers such a style means being a brother or a sister rather than a parent-figure; being a 'sharer' rather than a 'loner'. It means accepting the limitations that those you work with will place upon you . . . For congregations a collaborative style means taking responsibility, being allowed to be powerful, not being dependent on the person or group of persons, being engaged in ministry to the world.[27]

Gardner describes some conditions necessary for the success of collaborative ministry, and it is interesting to note that these conclusions by a Methodist are not significantly different from those arrived at by the report of the Catholic Bishops' Conference of England and Wales on collaborative ministry, *The Sign we Give*.[28] This approach also transcends denominationalism. For a group to work well, Gardner writes, collective and individual boundaries have to be set so that no one is swamped, and everyone is agreed on what he or she will contribute. Time should be given for the maintenance of the group, and pastoral care of each other.

Conflict, when it occurs, has to be faced rather than hidden, negotiating until a compromise is found, even seeking outside help if necessary. The sheer amount of difference between people, with their different understandings, experiences and priorities, including, as the Catholic report notes, a difference in ways of communicating between women and men, means that argument, even conflict, is likely to occur and its existence is not a weakness to be hidden. Decision-making will be shared, but leadership appropriate to the task, and not necessarily ordained, is required. *The Sign we Give* calls the leader 'moderator of the aspirations, plans and priorities of a community, always holding the common good before them'.

To continue with Gardner:

If . . . a leader is a good listener, is able to help others in the group to take responsibility, is ready sometimes to allow his own views to be overridden, then the team will be able to work in a collaborative style. If, however, the designated or assumed leader must always be in control, can only see things his way, cannot put himself in others' shoes and cannot allow himself to be led, then there is little

chance that the team will be able to develop a collaborative style of working.[29]

I have happily left this quotation in the male language of the
time in which it was expressed, but I cannot deny that there
are some women also who prize control.

Thus in the matter of collaborative ministry it is not individual charisma that counts in the long run, but steadiness,
patience and consideration. There is time too in the group for
laughter, relaxing, sharing a joke. The benefits of working
collaboratively Gardner sees as the disciplining of energies
(compared to their dissipation in solo ministry); the sharing
of problems; support for those carrying responsibilities; the
stimulation of minds; the humanizing of ministers who do
not, indeed cannot, present an invincible public persona; the
shared context of prayer and worship. These are considerable gains. Finally, as the Catholics say, and as all would
agree, collaborative ministry is not simply about the internal
good of the church. It is about mission, the church showing
the world by its actions the possibility of transformation and
of a diversity which does not negate unity.

What, then, of congregations? How is the mutuality of the
evolution to become real? Malcolm Grundy plots out one
possible course. He begins from the 'minister-dominated
congregation', which is a negative way of putting what some
people have given their lives to, but in the context of moving
towards something more collaborative is a description of
where one starts. What happens in such a church is that the
minister ministers to the people and the people want to be
ministered to: 'They are a type of clients to the minister. The
attitude of letting themselves be served predominates.' In this
model the minister has to try to satisfy everyone's needs and
wishes:

Each group in the congregation makes its own demands –
the minister should visit all the families, should take
communion to the sick and should spend time with each

old person. The minister has to offer interesting trips for young people, try to reconcile fighting married couples, prepare interesting services, edit the parish newsletter, raise money to repair the church, for the central funds and to give away. .

The first move away from such fallible efforts at omni-competence comes in what Grundy calls 'the compliant congregation with some participation':

Here is the beginning of shared ministry . . . There are lively debates in the church council. People are encouraged to form groups to organize tasks, and house groups take place around specified themes. The servers' group meets without the minister, as do the choir and mothers' group. The Adult Catechumenate welcomes newcomers.

The important thing at this stage, Grundy argues, is that the reduced role of the minister should be understood by all. This is not simply a case of the minister having more free time. So Grundy's next heading is 'a congregation which begins to think'. That thinking involves the relationship between what members are now doing in the church and their faith. 'They begin to enjoy their new responsibilities, but more than that they see what they are doing in terms of their Christian discipleship.' From the question 'What is going on in this congregation?' people may ('hopefully' says Grundy) move to questions like 'What are we here for? What is the church for?' Then the general question becomes: 'What kind of church is needed to support adult belief, spiritual development and Christian service?'

Thereafter a church may proceed to be 'a congregation of shared responsibilities':

Each person in the congregation begins to discover how they can offer themselves for service within the community of faith or in the wider world. They no longer see themselves as the helpers of the minister, or anyone else, but live with the joy of being called by Christ himself to work for the unfolding and realization of the Kingdom wherever they are called to be.[30]

---

## What is PA?

The term Participatory Appraisal (PA) describes a growing family of approaches and methods which enable local people to appraise and share their knowledge of life and local conditions, in order that they can analyse, plan and act on these ideas. Through PA both rural and urban communities are able to identify their own priorities and make their own decisions about the future. During the PA process, information comes from local people, is shared between them and owned by them ... Numerous case-studies have indicated that the quality of information shared amongst local people is highly reliable and valid.

Information for Participatory Appraisal Workshop,
Institute of Ecology and Resource Management,
Schools of Forestry and Ecological Science,
University of Edinburgh

---

According to Grundy the congregation then becomes 'a community of communities', no longer a collective 'large group'. Small communities are established so that 'faith and life are shared in human-sized communities'. Thus lay people discover their own vocation and mission within the church and there is 'a pastoral, priestly role for the minister which far exceeds any concept which could have been dreamed of in the early stages of this development of sharing'.

Grundy's series is not a blueprint, not least because for the purposes of presentation he accentuates the positive. But it does give some sense of what change by evolution would mean within a congregation. All manner of contingencies would intrude on the actual implementation, from unwilling church members to the need for lay training, which would become as important as clerical training. Unfortunate experiences may occur en route. After a shared service one commentator wrote: 'Given the choice I would rather be able to hear one voice than not be able to hear six.'[31]

There has to be some soul-searching and theological consideration before collaborative ministry may be endorsed. It would, I believe, have more validity if it had arisen from congregational pressure than if it is devised by clergy. On the other hand, the church may have so marginalized and silenced the laity that they are not in a position to spearhead change.

But change will not occur unless they want it, and share the vision, whether that is my vision of many small diverse communities each with their own degree of autonomy in what they do, or Grundy's vision of several virtually autonomous groups within the one local church. But again, when the lives of members of a congregation are being enlisted by clergy in the new vision, these clergy would do well to remember how full and how stressed these lives may be already. The difference between clergy-thinking in this regard, and quasi-lay-thinking is remarked upon by Johnston McKay who moved from parish ministry into religious broadcasting.

I confessed how much I was enjoying my weekends. I went further and said I had discovered how much weekends were necessary after five days in office and studio. . . . One thing I had learned was how different the weekly cycle was. When I was a parish minister I worked up to Sunday morning as the moment I had to prepare for. But now that I was not in a parish any more, I found that I still wanted to relax on a Sunday morning. I now started to get worked up for the week on a Sunday evening, when I began to forget the weekend and to think about what the week ahead involved . . . I now realize how unreasonable it was for me to have expected other people with a different work pattern to share the psychological consequences of mine.[32]

As a minister who is not in a parish I recognize the aptness of McKay's comment. The least that should be deduced from it is that no one should feel pressured – even pressured by the example of others – to offer their services, or feel a Christian failure if they do not on account of their own stressful lives. That does not deny the value of collaborative ministry, which may speak volumes about community, but it does mean that it should not be a clergy enthusiasm which sweeps all before it.

I have reservations also about the theology which is often invoked, namely that baptism is a summons to ministry. That could be only somewhat caricatured as clergy *telling* laity that it is their *duty* to minister since the church has baptized them. Their parents were probably not told that at the baptism. In 1994 the Church of Scotland put out a new *Book of Common Order*, and if baptism had that implication one would have expected it to appear. Yet the emphases in infant baptism are on God's love offered, on the Christian community as a home in which the child may grow up to make in time his or her own response of faith and love. That response may indeed include taking some responsibility within the church, but even confirmation is not styled to suggest that. The adult baptism rubrics make no suggestion of that either. If the Trade Descriptions Act applied to the churches, they would be in breach of it.

It could be argued that such services are still steeped in the individualism and conception of the faith as private, characteristic of an age which is passing away. But the point I wish to make is that *this* is the conception into which everyone at present in the church was baptized. It may well come as a surprise (to put it no higher) to find that ministry was implied in the act. Liturgies, of course, may be rewritten, and theologies of baptism rethought, though I am personally doubtful about the sacrament *effecting* vocation, as it would have to. The link of baptism, having the church as a home and participating in what the church does, may certainly be made. But, at the very least, in propounding the view whereby 'all the baptized participate directly in the priest-hood of Christ', if companionship with the laity is to be preserved, it must not come over as a clergy means of putting pressure on the laity, nor as the plain duty of every right-thinking church member.

I recognize that in writing this book I may seem to be telling churches and members that it is their duty to consider and work out the implications of 'God with us'. But my own conception of what I am offering is a possible vision of faith and practice which may (or may not) stir a response. An emphasis on 'with' can do no more, and that, after all, is how I understand God to act. If collaborative ministry may be introduced in clusters of church communities as companion-ship in action without breaking companionship on the way, then it may indeed be the visible form divine grace is seeking, and a visible enactment of God with us.

To move from this intensely communal conception of the church to speak of chaplaincies may seem odd, but they form one means of connection to and from what is going on out-side the communities, and may prevent their undue intro-spection. I belong to a church whose concern for ministry is mainly the 'territorial parish ministry'. In one sense this is both understandable and right, since the church has the privilege and responsibility of bringing 'the ordinances of religion' to every part of the country. In another sense, how-ever, this overwhelming emphasis on geography, on where people live, fitting enough in its day, now colludes with the reduction of religion to private life and is maintained at the expense of any emphasis on where people work, in industry, technology, business, hospitals, schools and universities, the armed forces and so forth, or where people 'land' – hospitals again, and prison.

There is a dual symbolic role for chaplaincies of all kinds at the moment which would not change as the church changes.

Chaplaincy is, on the one hand, the voice of the church in the workplace, prison or whatever. But on the other hand, and this is less perceived by churches at large, chaplaincy also has an input into the churches' self-understanding, reminding the church that God is concerned with all of life, whatever form it takes, and symbolizing to the church that there is no place where divine presence, encouragement and judgment are absent.

> The reverse side of Industrial Mission is, therefore, a kind of mission to the churches to keep them from being satisfied with domestic endeavours.[33]

Chaplaincy is one of the oldest established ways the church can be 'with' those most often outside it, so that it fulfils William Temple's description of the church as 'the only organization that exists for the sake of those who are not members of it'. The companionship motif fits the role very well, whether chaplains are companioning overworked doctors, anxious students or depressed prisoners. Here, again, companion is a good term, for it implies being with and walking with, yet with a space which allows each to be him/herself. 'Friend', on the other hand, would convey something more intimate than is desirable in such circumstances. Companionship has to do with support, encouragement, honesty and constancy, not only being there (presence) but being-with, which is more robust.

Companionship is not a model of church or chaplaincy behaviour which encourages conflict, but it does not preclude critical judgment. Chaplains are not merely passive onlookers. But conflict, in any case, is no longer seen as a way to achieve one's desires. The move away from a history of simple conflictual opposition can be seen in the new postmodern Trades Union Congress (TUC) stance. In words which echo much of what I have been saying concerning the churches John Monks, its General Secretary, comments:

[F]or the European Commission the watchword is 'negotiated flexibility'. Unions and employers are seen as partners in the management of change. For them agreement is
preferable to coercion. The TUC and our unions see their
future closely tied to such a positive model of co-operation.
Developing the role of social partnership in regulating
Britain's labour market along European lines is, therefore,
a central objective for us. This is a radical agenda, which
involves our unions helping to solve the problems of
people, employers and government. This will show how
trade unions add value for individuals as well as institutions and how the movement can be seen as part of the
solution to problems rather than being part of them.[34]

If a trade union leader can write of 'partnership' with
employers, and work within the conception of negotiated
flexibility, then the companionship of chaplains may be part
of, indeed a beacon for, this new style of working.

One of the large, impossible questions for chaplains is:
whom do we companion? Is it those in work or those becoming redundant? Is it management or those affected by their
decisions (in any situation short of Monks' partnership)? Is it
the Prison Governor, the staff, the inmates? The ideal answer
is that chaplains companion everyone, since all are people
whom God companions – even the rich, the successful, the
careless. In practice, of course, human resources, let alone
financial resources, are limited, so some area, or people, or
issues, will take priority. Yet even in that case, given

the image of Jesus incarnating the availability and accessibility of God at a time when God was thought to be
remote in the heavens . . . we are not free simply to rupture
companionship with anyone.[35]

Much more could be written of chaplaincy, but my main
concern here is its total relation to church life. Chaplaincy
is an instance of the mission of the church, but I have chosen

### A Chaplain in Bosnia

This was the systematic, discriminate, trashing of everything. Every house, every shed, every building, in the
towns, in the villages, in the middle of nowhere, everything was strewn out in the gardens, along the roads, anything vaguely useful was ruined and useless. I know what
[Hell] is like, because I've been there. It's a frozen waste-
land, where danger lies all around, from mines, treacher-
ous weather and demons. The demons are the [Bosnian]
soldiers picking over the trash, ransacking everything,
driving like possessed morons, setting fire to everything,
intimidating in the drunkenness and 'celebratory' weapon
firing.

So how will we celebrate Easter? . . . The real hope this
Easter is . . . where refugees are returning, where 'real'
people have appeared on the streets, where chimneys have
begun to smoke in houses with boards and sheeting at the
windows, where the soil is beginning to be cultivated . . .
This will be like the first Easter, with doubters, with perse-
cution and distrust, with a small number of people trusting and rejoicing. The threat from the Romans and the
dark memories of Good Friday will be there. The wrecked
cars and all the rubbish will make Golgotha continue to
be a place of fear and ugliness, and all will be fragile until
they truly celebrate Pentecost and be strong in the birth of
the new 'community'.

Fr Cooke, *Royal Army Chaplains Department Journal*,
Vol.36, No.1, January 1997, pp.25f.

to take it separately since in present practice it is not the
church corporately which is involved. Yet the churches could
be more involved than they currently are. Continuing

companionship with chaplains in terms of support and encouragement, rather than leaving them to get on with their solitary roles, could be greatly enhanced. The box describing an army chaplain's experience in Bosnia, gives some idea of how much debriefing and fellowship may be needed. Companionship does not imply that the churches may define a chaplain's role, nor tell a chaplain what to do in specific circumstances, for they are not in the chaplain's situation and have entrusted that person with that post. But the trust should not prelude listening, encouragement, prayer.

Further, churches have a lot to learn from chaplains, who are, as it were, their scouts in the world at large. Churches may hear what is actually going on in prisons or hospitals and glean notions of how to relate to it all. That would be particularly important if the church were to become a multiplicity of small communities, for sometimes, even now, churches may believe that in appointing chaplains they have done their bit for local or national society, and may otherwise concentrate on their domestic concerns. In that case chaplains could stir up churches to be alert to their public responsibilities in the service of the omnipresent God.

Churches may also gain insight for changes in their own life. Thus it has often seemed to me ill-advised of churches to criticize relationships in industry while intra-church relations have left much to be desired. But a church which has shaped itself round notions of with, companionship and partnership has a plausibility structure from which to encourage such relationships elsewhere – such as Monks' proposal.

This ends a sketch of what community and its ministry might mean. But the second part of this book is cumulative rather than linear. There are issues addressed here which have implications for later chapters, while they in turn reflect back on notions of community and ministry. Life in the church, as anyone belonging to a church knows, is not so tidy that it can be chopped into separate discrete linear sections.

# 7

# Postmodern Spirituality

'Postmodern spirituality' is an intentionally vague term. Here it will cover some consideration of the widely differing practices lumped together as New Age, and also the welcome revival of a more focussed Christian spirituality whose appeal is ever more widely felt. Both of these, each in its own way, offer the proverbial window of opportunity to churches in the process of change, especially if the churches at large (while they are still 'at large'), and not simply interested individuals, would take up seriously their possibilities.

> There is a revival of interest in the religious and the spiritual, yet it has largely passed the churches by. There is a great interest in the person of Jesus, yet the churches seem unable to meet this. There is a deep sense of the existence of God – variously understood – yet the churches seem unable to respond.[1]

Thus Martin Palmer on the churches and the New Age. His contention is that although the movement may have its 'sillier aspects', such as 'healing crystals, horoscopes, divination systems [and] esoteric teachings',[2] these phenomena have ancient religious roots and tend to reappear accompanying religious upsurges. The practices should not be demonized for they are not themselves demonic. Rather they are, so to speak, the froth on the religious wave, for their purpose is to put their users in touch with ultimate forces in control of what is happening. The very idea of 'ultimate forces' goes beyond all modernist conceptions: it does not offer the blank wall that scientific rationality set up against those who wished to speak of faith.

John Drane equally calls for a more discriminating approach to the New Age, with less blanket condemnation. The church's problem, he writes, in what is by now a familiar complaint, is that it capitulated to the 'new, self-confident, all-pervading world-view dominated by the progress of scientific reason, technology and materialism'.[3] This coheres yet again with Will Storrar's thesis that the churches wedded themselves to modernity, since that was the culture in which they existed and through which they had to make their message heard. As I have already said, it is not that the church was wrong *then*, but that as the cultural ethos is changing it would be wrong *now* to remain fixed in what was right for its day. The churches have lost their partner, modernity, which gave their intellectual stance credibility. I am the last person to denigrate the rational and the intellectual, and I am not proposing that they be banned from the churches. It is more a case that an emphasis on them was one-sided, and their justifying appeal has declined. So, now, if there is no change, 'if we only feed our minds, we will become spiritually deformed and disabled, and as a result those who know they need some transforming experience will look elsewhere'.[4]

Likewise Palmer, in a discussion on the churches' role in Europe, gives an account of why people look to sects rather than to churches to express their spirituality. Some of his reasons will not challenge the churches, but many will:

They feel that the churches are too rational, too integrated in society, too open to everyone; they too easily come up with mediocre solutions, their liturgy is too abstract and too verbal, not eschatological. Smaller, more exclusive, more demanding communities are preferred which are opposed to society, like the Beast of the Apocalypse. With their simplified dogma these sects provide a heightened sense of identity among their members, and often succeed in prompting them to a higher moral life. They have a simplified world-view and often give simplistic answers to life's big questions. There is an absolute leadership upon which members can lean. Finally their liturgy is less stereotyped, less rigid; they make use of more accessible symbols which make spontaneous participation easier.[5]

The New Age, according to Drane, is now 'probably the most predominant view among people today'.[6] He cites a surprising statistic: in Western Germany in 1989 there were 90,000 registered witches and 30,000 Christian clergy of all denominations. Even considering the small size of covens as opposed to the occasional large church the disparity in numbers is striking. Yet for the most part the reaction of the churches has been to ignore the movement, judging it to be heterodox, and too bizarre to be any threat, or to write it off as a media-driven quest for oddities. Alternatively they have taken arms against it, as if it were indeed a sea of trouble, 'heaping vitriolic condemnation on everything and everyone that can vaguely be labelled "New Age"'.[7]

But that will scarcely do. To ignore all New Age aspirations and practices is to withhold companionship from a large part of present culture which is already open to the idea of 'the Beyond in the midst'. To denounce it is to rupture any possibility of companionship. Yet companionship has to be understood as a robust relationship. To be 'with' people is not to endorse without argument everything they do, just as God's being with us does not preclude divine judgment on our own failings. But God's judgment occurs *within* the companioning relationship. Similarly church criticisms of the New Age have to be expressed within, and in a manner suitable to, the possibility of relationship and its continuance, on our side at least.

Companionship here will mean also discerning not only what may be rejected, but also what may be encouraged by, or even introduced into, the churches from New Age emphases, such as the priority of experience over reason, for these perceptions will help the churches to address the culture in which we now live. That does not imply that New Age tendencies will take over the churches, but that churches in their (hoped for) future diversity will include places where people in their search for what may be spiritually meaningful for them may find themselves fulfilled in Christ.

It is often complained that the New Age represents a 'pick and mix' form of religion – a little Buddhism here, a vague idea of the I-Ching there, bound together with notions of Human Potential. But there is a sense in which everyone's religion is picked and mixed, perhaps with Eastern Orthodox insights modifying the Western tradition, with some liberation theology emphases changing the perspective, or criticisms from feminist theology opening some men's eyes. There has never been one single, total, chemically pure version of Christianity. The debate recorded in Acts 15 over whether the Gentiles should be circumcised and obey the Jewish law witnesses to that.

It may be objected that the picking and mixing described above is at least done within the varieties of Christianity. But then, how are we to account for the differences of approach to the question of miracles since the rise of scholarly historical consciousness? Are modernist accommodations within Christian belief acceptable (scarcely discernible as picking and mixing) while postmodern approaches are treated as alien? Indeed the existence of contemporary picking and mixing is not the issue. Rather its existence is a call to see what is being picked, by whom, and why. Yoga may be the very thing for a stressed Christian businessman; Buddhism may be the avenue to respect for non-human creation. We need the humility to learn before we judge.

'The West is in the grip of what is effectively a religious revival' writes Palmer,[8] though, clearly that is not how many churches see it. Such revivals, Palmer argues, often occur at times of upheaval and change. Sometimes, to mark off the near future from the past, change is divided into ages, a distinction already made in the apocalyptic books in the

Bible, such as Daniel and Revelation. Within the history of the Christian church Joachim de Fiore in the twelfth century envisioned the Age of the Father, followed by the Age of the Son, with the Age of the Spirit about to dawn. From that perspective claims about the New Age are simply reverting to type. The 'New Age' itself is not new, and it is rather the embracing of diverse practices, the 'channelling' of messages from unseen powers, the belief that God is human potential writ large, which require first understanding, then companionable critique.

On the other hand there is much to learn from the New Age. Much of it stands out against the contemporary emphasis on the individual, on competition as the way to behave, on institutional structures dominating life, on shopping as the chief end of woman. Many are also actively concerned about the state of the environment. These are all issues on which the churches could make common cause, if they were not afraid to be sullied by New Age contact, for the same impulses are felt within the church as outside it. It is not as if church members were pure Enlightenment products while the ferment goes on elsewhere. In that respect it is interesting to read David Bosch writing on new paradigms for the church in mission, but sounding almost like a New Ager himself:

A basic reorientation is thus called for. One should, again, see oneself as a child of Mother Earth and as sister and brother to other human beings. One should think holistically, rather than analytically, emphasize togetherness rather than distance, break through the dualism of mind and body, subject and object, and emphasize 'symbiosis'.[9]

What is perhaps more serious than the 'pick and mix' attitudes of New Agers is their propensity for taking up a subject or a religion, skimming its surface and dropping it again as the personal mélange changes. From the church's side there are plenty of calls for single conviction and commitment instead. But in the first place it has to be understood how foreign such demands seem for someone who has known nothing but a consumer society where one has to be futuristic to be trendy, for even this season's fashions are incipiently passé. In the second place such lack of intellectual depth is not reason enough for Christians to dissociate themselves from such people. Commitment may not be demanded in the first place, although it may be learned en route. Changes in expectation, at least initial expectation, is part of ministering to present culture.

One virtue of postmodern thinking is that it calls for the recognition of the 'other', of others, of plurality of cultures, diversity of languages, multiplicity of logics, the wealth and variety of meaning produced by cultures existing side by side. In contrast to what happens in the socio-economic and political system where we have a hierarchy based on power relations, in the cultural field we find heterogeneity that can only be properly understood when it is seen as diversity expressing itself on a footing of equality.

J. de Santa Ana, 'Cultures in Tension and Dialogue', *International Review of Mission*, January 1996, p.98

Martin Palmer concludes his book on much the same note of an interaction between Christianity and what propels and invigorates the New Age. He has a vision of Christianity, having learned from the New Age, as happily diverse, 'capable of transporting us with joy, of placing us at risk and asking us to look hard at the wrong-doing and violence which we inflict upon ourselves and each other'.[10] The New Age is not notable for its emphasis on sin. But even here Palmer suggests it has something to teach the churches, namely that we learn to forgive ourselves and others, in order to grow within the purposes of God for creation.

I believe that the Christianity that is emerging will lose most of its hierarchy, will be able to tell its story and the story of life in vividly different ways and will have taken on board many new ideas, shapes and forms from the diversity of faiths and cultures which it is encountering.[11]

In the process of coming to terms with the New Age and the various spiritual programmes offered, the churches are bound to make mistakes from time to time. The process will always need challenging and changing. But finally there is no more a completely novel New Age now than in any generation, and the Christian response is not to oppose or stagnate, but to live out its active, life-changing belief in Christ's words: 'Behold I make all things new.'

The hum of excited spiritual exploration within the New Age is very different from the 'melancholy, long, withdrawing roar' (Matthew Arnold) of the attitude which Noel Davies, writing of Wales, calls a spirituality of decline with a crisis of faith inside as well as outside the churches.

Many are more and more convinced that the powers ranged against the churches in Wales are too great to resist. We are in danger, as a result, of being imprisoned by a spirituality of decline which foresees only further decline and seeks only the resources to maintain present church patterns and structures for as long as possible. This is not a formula for renewal.[12]

The churches in Wales are not alone in feeling powerless to arrest decline and therefore continuing to minister as before to the remnant. But the tenor of this book is that the churches face an opportunity here and now, and that, if they disengage from the more Byzantine structures of their present organizational framework; if they diversify the range of their communal, liturgical and practical activities; if they keep in touch with what is happening in present culture; if, above all, they live out and manifest the relationships initiated by God with us, they will at the very least have spoken a word in season for the present time, which is the scope of anyone's responsibility. Life-long commitment to a habit of church-going may no longer be a prominent cultural feature, but churches will have to encourage some involvement with their message rather than giving in to a simple lament for the past.

One of the hopeful signs beyond a spirituality of decline is the increased interest in Christian spirituality which has much to offer people searching. A recent Letter on Evangelism from the WCC took this as its starting point:

> Millions of people the world over are showing an interest in religious experience, mysticism and spirituality to such a degree today that scholars of social and cultural change are taking notice and making it one of their main discussion points.[13]

The indications of its increasing importance are there for anyone to see. Books, CDs and tapes of mystical and spiritual experience have huge sales. Pilgrimages, visits to holy places and involvement in monastic sites have made a startling come-back. Seminars, retreats and courses on spirituality multiply.

Much more of this could be made by the churches, endorsing the move, advertising (literally – and including New Age outlets) its benefits. But where spirituality has not been part of their mainstream tradition churches remain largely ignorant of its possibilities and reluctant to give it a high profile. And in this, as in other matters, churches are about as easy to turn round as oil-tankers. Yet in corners of Protestant churches, and on a larger scale in the Roman Catholic Church and parts of Anglicanism, spirituality is becoming steadily more important.

Some are wary of this development as an apparent retreat from urgent issues of justice and peace into self-absorbed introspection.

A narrow spirituality refuses to recognize the interdependence and wholeness of life; its concern rejects involvement, and its preoccupation with individual piety derives from the false assumption that the individual soul is more open to change than social institutions.[14]

---

### Spirituality as Prayer

The need is for a form of prayer which combines both depth and responsive action. God must be encountered in the public sphere as well as the private sphere, and the two must inform each other. The forms of prayer are hugely varied: lighting candles, using a kneeler, repeating the 'Jesus prayer', writing prayers in reflective mode, taking intentional devotional walks through the community, praying with media such as clay or paint, singing or chanting prayer, and of course the essence of all prayer – silence before God.

M. Riddell, *Threshold of the Future*, SPCK 1998, p.137

---

Certainly some seekers after spirituality are concerned only with the state of their own souls. But even then, the process is usually to make that soul more open and responsive than to shut it up in its own internal convolutions. The monk Thomas Merton, whose books on the contemplative life are very popular, endorses that view. After a consideration of some of the grave social situations in the world he continues:

In such a situation it is no longer permissible for Christians seriously and honestly to devote themselves to a spirituality of evasion, a cult of other-worldliness that refuses to take account of *the inescapable implication of all men* in the problems and responsibilities of the nuclear age . . . Lack of interest in the desperate fate of man is a sign of culpable insensitivity, a deplorable incapacity to love! It cannot in any sense claim to be Christian. It is not even genuinely human.[15]

For John Bell of the Iona Community also spirituality 'is not chiefly concerned with prolonging states of ecstasy, rapture or private religious intensity', although all these may be experienced. Bell's own metaphor is 'oil'.

[T]he oil which fuels the machinery by which we relate to God, to God's world and to God's people . . . It pervades all of life and is not simply the preserve of special moments in sacred places . . . All the true saints of God never got what they wanted, did what they liked, or lived on cloud nine. So when we, in our present cultural context, wish to define or distinguish the role and purpose of spirituality, it is not to legitimize escapism. It is to enable flaccid hedonists to face up to what they would rather avoid.[16]

Such spirituality consists in a disciplined remembering of God's history-long companionship and our own potentialities within that history. Further there is an equally disciplined waiting on God, foregoing the instant fix or the effortless relationship. Then there is disciplined imagination of the future, which could be compared to Martin Luther King's 'I have a dream'. All of that takes time, all are ongoing throughout life, and the results may transform relationships with God and with other people. It is hard to imagine any church objecting to that process, and clear that they stand to gain from its enlargement. Merton's Catholic background to spirituality is different from the Presbyterian Bell's, but the emphasis on discipline and the relation to action are the same:

A certain depth of disciplined experience is a necessary ground for fruitful action. Without a more profound human understanding derived from exploration of the inner ground of human existence, love will tend to be superficial and deceptive. Traditionally the ideas of prayer, meditation and contemplation have been associated with this deepening of one's personal life and the expansion of the capacity to understand and serve others.[17]

---

*Metaphors for a Spiritual Director*

A host provides a guest a resting place for deeper self-exploration.

A friend accompanies a confidant on a contemplative journey.

A teacher shares with a student the wisdom of spiritual and human development.

A guide assists a believer in avoiding the pitfalls often found along the journey.

A midwife assists a birthgiver to go through periods of desolation and celebrates with her the

birthing of new life.

E. P. C. Tam, 'Spiritual Direction' in
*Dictionary of Pastoral Studies*, SPCK forthcoming

---

Spirituality, then, has to do with the quality of life as it is lived. From that point of view it is understandable that Celtic spirituality has proved attractive. For, as Esther de Waal writes:

What they said and sung – for these prayers were also hymns and poetry – grew out of their sense of the presence of God as the most immediate reality in their lives. Religion permeated everything they did. They made no distinction between the secular and the sacred. They were unable to discern boundaries of where religion began and ended and thus found it natural to assume that God was lovingly concerned in everything they did.[18]

The relation between this way of thinking and a theology of God with us is evident.

> God bless to me the new day
> Never vouchsafed to me before;
> It is to bless thine own presence
> Thou hast given me this time, O God.
>
> Bless thou to me mine eye,
> May mine eye bless all it sees;
> I will bless my neighbour
> May my neighbour bless me.
>
> God, give me a clean heart,
> Let me not from sight of thine eye;
> Bless to me my children and my wife,
> And bless to me my means and my cattle.
>
> *Carmina Gadelica* collected and translated
> by Alexander Carmichael (1900),
> Floris Books 1994, p.79

Enjoyment is one of the strands in Celtic spirituality, and Allchin urges that spirituality leads to celebration, which occurs when all the divisions in humanity promoted in modernity are overcome.

The opposites which need to come together for celebration are of many kinds: heart and head, feeling and thinking:

conscious and unconscious, critical intellect and intuitive intellect.

Further, in all this reunion, the body, so often in Christianity considered as base matter to be denied and transcended, becomes something to include in relationship with God.

> [T]he way spirituality is to be followed anew in a time of changing consciousness . . . will involve a new discovery of the place of the body and the life of the senses in our whole approach to God, our fellow men, and the world around us. It is through the whole of human nature that God works.[19]

It was not always so in spirituality, for here also flourished what Sallie McFague has called the 'western preference for the abstract, the universal and the disembodied'.[20] Yet McFague comments elsewhere on the 'surprisingly "bodily" tradition' which Christianity is, or could be

> not only because of the resurrection of the body but also because of the bread and wine at the eucharist as the body and blood of Christ, and the church as the body with Christ at its head.[21]

Moreover she urges the perception that 'God loves bodies'.

In these various ways postmodern spirituality has developed a much greater freedom than it had in the Catholic practices of the 1960s. At that point Rahner found that even spirituality was prescribed and dictated, and that curtailed an individual's free interaction with God. In that situation he had to stand up for personal freedom in personal piety.

> Every existing form of piety presented to my choice, as it were, from outside, may be considered under the aspect of the externally inflicted law . . . All these . . . confront me with something which is already there . . . they at least

appeared to limit my spirituality which is obviously the most intimate realization of my freedom. Now if personal freedom is basically a unique gift of God, what we call spirituality must have an inner connection with it. Hence the institutional norms of the church and the freedom which is realized most decisively in the spiritual life cannot be in complete harmony from the beginning.[22]

What is wanted, then, is neither a narrow, self-regarding piety nor an imposed, and to that extent mechanical, method of spirituality. Instead spirituality may bring about growth in the individual's self-understanding in relationship with God which impels involvement wherever God is at work. When, then, there is spiritual hunger among church members, or in society at large, it should be possible to hope from churches of the future that the need will be expected and recognized – indeed felt by most – and that there will be well-known, well-endorsed places where such hunger can be satisfied and to which others from outside the church may come to discover and participate in Christian spiritual enrichment.

# 8

# Peace and Justice

On the whole it is far less difficult to persuade churches as institutions that they should be active on social issues of peace and justice than it is to recommend that spirituality should have a higher profile within the total diversity. There has been an activist strain in most Western churches, highly visible in the WCC, which is admirable in itself. Sometimes one may wonder, however, whether that enthusiasm serves to cover a late-modern style of spiritual vacuum, or whether it is there to bridge theological differences. There is an old adage: doctrine divides; action unites. Whatever the motivation, however, the notion of companionship with the marginalized, the dispossessed, the near invisible fringes of society has been developed with commitment by effective groups within most church families.

Yet at the same time there are forces in Western society, felt equally within the churches, which militate against such active concern, forces which may keep the numbers of the actively concerned to very small groups within any particular local church. The desire to be comfortable, and for that comfort not to be disturbed, remains a strong temptation. Kenneth Galbraith has written of a 'culture of contentment' massaged by financial and professional security and indulged by easy consumerism.

The old classes, whose conflict Marx prophesied, have almost disappeared, but in their place Galbraith discerns the comfortably situated on the one hand, and on the other 'a large number of less affluent or even impoverished who do the work and render the services that make life pleasant'.[1]

The postmodern equivalent of the one-time industrial pro-
letariat are the providers of service for those who can afford
them. But even the service providers are at least employed. So
there remains a danger for churches of what was the middle
class that social contentment may breed a desire not to be
disturbed over issues of peace and justice, or to be satisfied
with the occasional donation to good causes.

A further Western temptation to remain uninvolved may
be drawn from Neil Postman's analysis in *Amusing Ourselves
to Death*. Here Postman contrasts the prophetic warnings of
George Orwell in *1984* with Aldous Huxley's *Brave New
World*. Orwell feared that externally imposed oppression in
the form of Big Brother would overcome freedom. Huxley, on
the other hand, wrote as if pleasure and distraction would be
more subtly and potently subversive. While Orwell feared
that by 1984 books would be banned, Huxley foresaw a
brave new world in which no one would be bothered to read
a book.

> Orwell feared those who would deprive us of information.
> Huxley feared those who would give us so much that we
> would be reduced to passivity and egoism. Orwell feared
> that the truth would be concealed from us. Huxley feared
> that the truth would  be drowned in a sea of irrelevance.
> Orwell feared we would become a captive of culture, Hux-
> ley feared we would become a trivial culture, preoccupied
> with some equivalent of the feelies, the orgy-porgy and the
> centrifugal bumblepuppy.[2]

As long as there was an opposing power in the old Soviet
Union, interpreted along Orwellian lines, his prophecies held
credibility. But in the contemporary West Huxley's has more
force. What may keep society at large, and many church
members, contented is economic security enlivened by trivial
pursuits.

Comfort and contentment is the form self-sufficiency takes
in contemporary culture. Its devotees require no father or

home of unconditional love because they know no brokenness or insecurity. They are equally well-padded against
a need for God as intimate friend through life's better or
worse, or as a challenging travelling companion through life's
changes. Yet, having said all that in general terms, there are
still shattering experiences which even the most comfortable
individuals may undergo. And at the same time, of course,
there is poverty and homelessness, ill-health and poor housing at home, while in the world at large there is war, famine,
landmine injuries, displacement, and much more.

---

### The Free Market Economy

Even George Soros, the international financier, asserts
that unless the uninhibited pursuit of self-interest is 'tempered by the recognition of a common interest that ought
to take precedence over particular interests, our present
system is liable to break down'. While there may be an
understandable reluctance to move too quickly to join Mr
Soros, when an eminent capitalist criticizes the system,
should not the churches find a way to utilize and maxi-
mize that? Are there not committed Christian business
people who could join with the church in devising ways to
mitigate the negative effects of the free market economy
and allow all to share in its benefits? Without some new
initiatives how will the churches move beyond making
statements and secure the necessary expertise to persuade
people to take corrective action?

R. L. Turnipseed, 'Missional Responses in the Changing US
Context', *International Review of Mission*, October 1998,
p.532, citing G. Soros, 'The Capitalist Threat', *Atlantic
Monthly*, February 1997

---

Moltmann makes a striking picture of the 'rich', in whatever ways they are rich, as those whose hands are closed,
grasping their possessions, while the poor, however they are

poor, have their hands open. Poverty thus implies both dependence and openness, while the rich 'are neither dependent on others nor open for others'.

> 'Poverty' . . . extends from economic, social and physical poverty to psychological, moral and religious poverty. The poor are all those who have to endure acts of violence and injustice without being able to defend themselves. The poor are all who have to exist physically and spiritually on the fringe of death, who have nothing to live for and to whom life has nothing to offer. The poor are all who are at the mercy of others, and who live with empty and open hands.

Thus 'poverty' has economic, circumstantial and religious dimensions. 'Riches' are equally multi-dimensional, running from the results of exploitation and social superiority to the attitude which 'does not want to have to say thank-you to anyone for anything'.

> What is meant is an attitude, and the thing it depends on. What is meant are possessions and the violence through which they are acquired and maintained. 'The rich' are all the people who live with tightly-clenched hands.[3]

Many, though not all, of the ills of contemporary British society have to do with poverty. Here I am concerned with its existence rather than with its causes and instances, for there is already a wealth of literature on that subject. I am more concerned here to consider relationships, and the implications of God being with us, such that 'with' is the term of relationship which defines what the church is like and what it does. That is also a constant reminder that God has no favourites, that God who is with us in church is also and simultaneously loving those outside unconditionally. The world of the poor is not alien territory to God.

Two kinds of relationship may be dismissed pretty quickly

as not exemplifying 'with'. The first is the occasional giving of money to beggars and the homeless who increasingly occupy our streets. That does not mean that nothing should be given to such people; rather it means that nothing is solved by such tokens.

[T]he relationship between a beggar and the person from whom he solicits alms is so structured as to make virtually impossible an authentic, caring relationship. The passer-by is invited to give a paltry sum as a kind of bribe to persuade the beggar to go away and terminate the embarrassing relationship. There is no way within the encounter of meeting the beggar's deeper needs, which are, as with everyone, for care, respect, affection and a recognition of worth as well as for material resources.[4]

That example is fairly clear. What is less clear is that enthusiastic middle-class endeavours to 'go in there and empower the poor' may be equally ineffective and mask a subtle kind of imperialism – the kind which knows in advance what is good for its recipients. Margaret Walsh engagingly describes her own process of enlightenment.

We went to live and work in the inner city with great dreams to empower and liberate. Local people began to discover the benevolent Hope Community, knowing that we had that extra tin of beans and a blanket or two. We soon were battling with a dependency mentality, born from ever-increasing hardship and a hopeless lack of self-esteem. The temptation was great. It gave us the opportunity to play 'Ladies Bountiful' and to be in control over people's lives at a very basic level. Soon, however, we also came to know the looks of resentment.[5]

Part of the problem was that members of the Community arrived thinking they had the skills needed for counselling and social analysis and could simply put these into practice.

It took time for them to realize the need to listen to their neighbours rather than impose an agenda for empowerment. Then the local community, with encouragement and support, organized opposition to a local lead-polluting factory. At that point the relationship became more 'with' than 'for':

> During the course of this action I began to realize more and more that our most important achievements were when local people began to grow in self-esteem and realize their own potential.[6]

But beyond all ameliorative endeavours, the bottom line is that poverty excludes. It excludes from fullness of life, range of choice, the benefit of health and the possibility of work. Kenith David enlarges this to give types of exclusion world-wide, together with their dismissive categorizations which all too easily deny relationship:

economic exclusion – 'the useless'
political exclusion – 'the usual suspects'
social exclusion – 'the unwanted'
cultural exclusion – 'the backward'
Third World exclusion – 'the underdeveloped'[7]

To that one might add physical exclusion – 'the handicapped'.

There are, however, entirely practical arguments against tolerating the continuation of poverty. It is costly in social security benefits; it is wasteful in the non-development of skills and talents; it is threatening in the social disorder it may bring about. A whole new industry in home protection with alarms, floodlights and window locks has grown up in Britain to meet that fear of potential violence. But if poverty is manifested in exclusion from positive economic and social structures it will not be enough for the churches to work to enhance the self and social esteem of the poor here and there, though that in itself is no mean feat, and could lead the newly confident to challenge 'the system'. Some form of political involvement may well become necessary.

Decisions made by such bodies as Central or Local Government either enhance my dignity and integrity as a human being and a child of God or they impair and restrict it. So, too, they enhance or impair the life of the local community of which I am a part. In short, these institutional activities either enable or block the coming of the Kingdom of God. A very large part of the exercise in power and the control of resources is, in fact, the political process of the society and world in which we live. It seems to be that, whether I like it or not, both I and my parishioners are bound up in a political process which we cannot avoid.[8]

Active involvement in politics, however, particularly in a demand for change, requires good information and organization, which are often beyond any church's competency to acquire on its own. There is value, therefore, in joining work already being done by others. Greenwood describes such action as a possibility for a single parish:

An Anglican priest who is a probation officer helped us to see that it would be impertinent and patronizing for us, full of new fervour, to begin setting up Christian structures to *look after* the 'poor' of the council estate. Far better for us to listen and observe where the community police constable had been beaten up, where the tenants already have an association, where community workers are in conversation with glue- and alcohol-abusers, where there is a local transport committee, a group for single parent families, old people's lunch clubs, Samaritans, marriage guidance and the like, and offer to lend talent and support to what they are achieving.[9]

Further, Greenwood has a word of warning for church activists who see themselves in a morally clear light in relation

to the distribution of wealth. His comments concern the
Church of England, but have reference to all churches which
have acquired funds.

It is easy to be pious about the organized church's spiritual
contribution to the nations, whilst forgetting completely
that it is only the deft handling of investments by the
Church Commissioners at Millbank, with all the ethical
minefields inevitably involved, that makes it possible to
finance clergy stipends, pensions and housing. The World
and the Church cannot be too simplistically divided:
creation and stewardship of wealth in order to be the
church and do mission brings its own tangled web of
decisions and priorities.[10]

All the churches and their clergy share this ambiguity to
some extent. No one's hands are entirely clean if they profit
at all from the status quo. But that does not mean that there
should be no involvement. The church's being is being with
God and with other people. Neither reluctance nor false
modesty should stand in the way. Inaction itself is a form of
activity in relation to social ills. That, as Segundo writes, has
become particularly clear in Latin America, but is equally
true of Britain.

Everything about our life – our security, our nourishment,
our leisure – depends upon the maintenance of a social
order which we may not see, but which has become as
close and indispensable to us as the air we breathe. Unlike
the air, however, the social order is never neutral. To sit
quietly at home is to adopt a public stance which can mean
life or death, nourishment or hunger, justice or exploitation for other human beings. And if we are Christians, it
means something to God too.[11]

The discussion in this chapter so far has been very general,
as indeed must much of the consideration in this part of the

book, which is primarily exploring areas in which withness – with God and with other people – may be exercised by the churches, while the actual practice will be dependent on local situations. But peace and justice concerns go beyond the local, and in this instance I wish to sketch two areas in which the churches' voice may be heard, and more justifiably heard, since demands for the ethical investment of church funds have been more generally raised.

The first is the issue of landmines, which Britain had a long history of manufacturing. The International Committee of the Red Cross estimates that eight hundred people a month are killed by mines while another twelve hundred are maimed. If we have no sense of companionship with the people of Angola, Cambodia, Kurdistan and the Sudan, to name only four of the countries affected, then we may find the statistic regrettable, but beyond our concerns or capacity for action.

Statistics alone may be cold numbers. But each of them represents a human tragedy. A visitor to Cambodia, keeping strictly to a cleared road, records her conscientization on seeing a one-legged farmer with his young daughter on a farm surrounded by 'beware mines' signs. These went round his vegetable plot, his path to the water pump and his access to the road. The family lived surrounded by mines.

> We were told not to take any risks, but what choice did they have? Having to flee conflict after conflict, letting armies shell the fields, drive tanks through the waterways and finally lay mines on any penetrable piece of land . . . But why do they stay? Where else do they have to go? Who will take them in? . . . In a country stricken with poverty who will employ a one-legged farmer, or with what resources can he move his family to safer ground? . . . How long will it be before a de-mining team arrives in their area to liberate them from the silent killers?[12]

The 1997 Ottawa Treaty on Landmines – or to give it its full title, the Convention on the Prohibition of the Use,

Stockpiling, Production and Transfer of Anti-personnel
Mines and on their Destruction – came into force in 1999,
though many of the signatory states have not yet ratified it,
and many aggressive states have not even signed it.

---

### The Landmine Treaty

Together we have begun to map out a way for the international community to move forward together in a coherent
and co-ordinated way to promote and ensure the speedy
and effective entry-into-force and ongoing implementation of the new convention ... I would also like us to
remind ourselves that this was just the beginning. It is an
ongoing commitment to partnership and co-operation
that will enable us to succeed in meeting our goal of a
world finally freed from the fear and suffering of anti-
personnel mines.

Lloyd Axworthy, Canadian Minister of Foreign Affairs,
Closing Speech, Ottawa, 4 December 1997

---

The churches were involved in this issue long before it
achieved a high profile when Diana, Princess of Wales
became involved. It is, perhaps, a comment on British society
that the suffering became truly media-worthy only when
the most newsworthy member of the royal family took up
the case. I am not aware of any television programmes on the
subject, for instance, since her death. But for some time there
has been an International Campaign to Ban Landmines and
of the one thousand organizations involved twenty-five per
cent are church-related. Its co-ordinator, Ms Jody Williams,
received the Nobel Peace Prize in 1997.

What, then, may the churches do now? The UK has begun
dismantling its own stock of landmines, but it has moved
much more slowly in the matter of removing the mines
already laid. Further, in the recent wars in Yugoslavia anti-

tank mines and cluster bombs were used, both of which may be just as damaging to civilians returning after the war. The Ottawa Treaty remains only a beginning. So campaigns to raise awareness, like the one to remove debt from impoverished countries, and perhaps invoking Princess Diana, may be mounted with the general public, MPs and the media through direct representations, meetings, prayer vigils and so forth. It will not be easy for the UK government to move further since jobs depend on the armaments industry. Yet, put in the balance with the lives lost, or rendered virtually useless by the products, the jobs issue pales into insignificance. That does not mean that the churches would break off all companionship with those who are made redundant, and leave them to sink or swim, but here, as so often in critical moral issues, it is not possible for everyone to win all the time.

---

The South Korean and US government's official position that anti-personnel landmines in the DMZ (demilitarized zone) are necessary to prevent a possible North Korean invasion to the South reflects . . . an unchanging cold war mentality and unwillingness to pursue peace and reunification in the peninsula. There are currently 1,000,000 anti-personnel landmines scattered along the DMZ which at this time are killing mainly soldiers. The presence of the landmines is threatening the lives of civilians who live near the DMZ as well as destroying the surrounding local ecosystem . . . PROK urges all churches and persons of all faiths and creeds to support the complete and immediate ban on anti-personnel landmines in the Korean peninsula and throughout the world.

From a statement on landmines by the Presbyterian Church in the Republic of Korea (PROK) 1997

Out of his great humanity Bishop Desmond Tutu has encapsulated the distress and the complicity in the matter of landmines in a prayer:

Lord, how can I serve you without arms?
How can I walk in your way without feet?
I was collecting sticks for the fire when I lost my arms.
I was taking the goats to water when I lost my feet.
I have a head, but my head does not understand why
     there are landmines in the grazing land, or why
     there is a trip wire across the dusty road to the market.

My heart is filled with a long ache.
I want to share your pain, but I cannot.
You look at me but I cannot bear your gaze.
The arms factory provides a job for my son,
and my taxes paid for the development of 'smart' bombs.
I did not protest when soldiers planted fear into the earth
     that smothers the old people and the anxious mothers
     and fills the young men with hate.

Lord, we are all accomplices in the crime of war
which is a lust for power at all costs.
The cost is too much for humanity to bear.
Lord, give us back our humanity, our *ubuntu*.
     Teach us to serve you without arms.

Another area for possible action on peace and justice is the matter of what are often now called 'uprooted people'. On 2 April 1999 *The Guardian* newspaper contained an article by John Vidal entitled 'The Endless Diaspora', building on British concern over the then current nightly television showing of lines of Kosovars forced to flee their country. But the issue of refugees and the internally displaced is far larger than that. Indeed a conservative estimate is that 25,000,000 have had to leave their countries with another 25,000,000 forced from their homes yet still within their country.

Mexico has up to 100,000 Guatemalans in exile; the Ivory Coast took in up to 700,000 fleeing the civil war in Liberia; Nepal contains around 115,000 refugees from Bhutan and Tibet; a million have been displaced in Sri Lanka; Sudan has refugees from Ethiopia and Ethiopia has refugees from Sudan, as well as others from Kenya and Somalia. And these are just a few of the twenty-six countries from Bosnia to Angola where this problem exists.

Small wonder that there is now a High Commissioner for refugees at the United Nations. She reports the increased use of mass evictions in order to establish an ethnically or culturally homogeneous society. And who suffers most? Vidal's answer is:

> Minority groups, the already stateless, indigenous populations and others in poor or medium poor countries who have little or no representation.

Paradoxically, in some countries where people would like to leave, such as Sri Lanka, the powers of both government and opposition forcibly prevent them in a move to maintain control.

> The lot of the refugee or displaced person is increasingly hard. Globally there is mounting rejection of refugees and states have been quick to erect physical and administrative barriers. On top of the physical and emotional pain, asylum seekers may spend years in fear of expulsion, may be denied the right to settle permanently, to work, be disqualified from welfare benefits or be kept in detention, or, most often in the poorest countries, in camps.

The *Guardian* article outlines the problem. But what can churches do, even churches convinced first of the omnipresence of God, so that God accompanies all these uprooted people, and then of their own responsibility for companionship? There seem to me to be two answers here. One is to support the work of the WCC (or relevant Catholic bodies) as a non-governmental organization (NGO) involved in the welfare and return of uprooted people; the other is to welcome and stand with refugees, migrants and other displaced people arriving in this country.

---

### How to Respond to a Crisis: Rwanda

After a short-term pilot project, African Community Initiative Support Teams (ACISTs) were set up. Instead of bringing in outside 'trauma experts' these teams used and supported the resources available in the community. They identified people already working with the traumatized and supported them. Each ACIST team comprised two people – one African and one expatriate – equipped with a vehicle and a radio. They had small funds for emergency projects and worked directly with community leaders, not national structures . . . Such an approach achieved immediate practical results. It also addressed the issue of abandonment by introducing an international presence to witness to the past and to the present. By building confidence in individuals, people could begin to contemplate rebuilding their own communities.

*Commitment to Jubilee:*
*Strategies for Hope in Times of Crisis,*
WCC Programme on Sharing and Service 1999, p.32

---

The Sharing and Service Unit of the WCC has devoted much time and consideration to the plight of all uprooted people, of all faiths and none. Its means are networking and advocacy, that is, working *with* even when speaking *for*, and urging local involvement over international intervention.

At the United Nations [the WCC's] Sharing and Service advocates for assistance to people caught in emergencies. It advocates for ways of working that recognize the dignity and strength of communities – even when they are in crisis.[13]

Unlike the common notion of intervention from the outside with a 'peace initiative', the WCC upholds where possible the value of local resources to restore peace.

It works by first identifying issues at local or national levels with partner churches or groups. It then brings many of these issues to regional or international levels where policies, agreements or Conventions may need to be changed or involved. As this is achieved, the national/local partners are able to use them in their own advocacy.

Out of this has come much consciousness-raising and some success. Through much patient negotiation in both Mexico and Guatemala, with refugees themselves and with the Guatemalan government, the WCC, with the assistance of other relevant interchurch organizations, helped to engineer the return of thousands of Guatemalan refugees (those who wanted to go back) to their own country.

[The process] has demonstrated that dialogue in such a forum can provide solutions to a multitude of problems, both political and logistical. It also shows that such a mechanism can form part of the very initial, and still vulnerable, processes that are contributing to the creation of peace in Guatemala.

There may be occasions when utter intransigence makes armed intervention necessary, but the pattern of patient negotiating, of not losing connections with either the refugees or the government of a country makes fewer wounds, involves less loss of face for those in power, and therefore may lead more quickly to stabilization. This is companionship showing its worth at an international level.

With 25,000,000 refugees abroad in the world it is impossible that Britain will not be affected. The government, fearful of 'economic migrants' hoping to tap into a better life in the UK, tightened its controls, though in 1999 these were partially relaxed. I shall quote from the Church of Scotland's 1997 booklet *Welcoming the Refugee: agenda for congregations*, but similar protests were made from other churches.

In 1996 the General Assembly expressed the deepest regret at the steps taken by HM Government in the face of concerted opposition of the churches and other bodies directly concerned, to withdraw benefit from asylum seekers and increase controls and restrictions relating to immigration and asylum, and called on HM Government to treat those seeking asylum in Britain generously, compassionately, efficiently and sensitively. Sadly the protest and plea fell on deaf ears and the position of asylum seekers has worsened in the intervening time, with many now in a situation of desperate need.

The situation is regularly under review and some amelioration has occurred since 1997, but the major difficulties remain.

The Church of Scotland booklet offered a number of ways in which a congregation could help a refugee, such as prayer support, befriending and offering practical help. Co-operation with local Councils of Churches and the local community was advised, with special help from the Scottish Refugee Council. All this again is companionship in action, and it may climax in offering sanctuary in cases of special need. But giving sanctuary is not to be entered on lightly, and its issues should be discussed within the church.

People need to know the legal position (sanctuary is not recognized as a right in Scots Law), what the procedures are and what the difficulties may be, but they also need to have the opportunity to consider and discuss the principles of this

particular kind of support and their own moral or theological position. That process maintains companionship
within the church as well as in relation to the refugee. The
possibility of dissent has to be met – just as God's companionship and influence towards action may meet with our
own dissent. And sanctuary itself can never be more than a
stop-gap. But it may serve to give a breathing-space, allowing
more time to put a case together, and it attracts publicity to
the issue.

---

### Dutch churches make asylum-seekers a national issue

In a rare example of united action the main churches of
the Netherlands have come out in public opposition to the
Dutch government's treatment of asylum-seekers and have
set up a camp-site for them in Duringeloo . . . The initiative has prompted extensive coverage and an intense
national debate in the Dutch media, resulting in the
involvement of government officials. The first reaction of
most politicians was to condemn the church initiative as a
'public relations' exercise. Churches should not get
involved in politics, they said. Elizabeth Schmitz, parlia-
mentary undersecretary for refugees, promised to seek
new solutions for those refugees unable to leave the
Netherlands. After an intense debate in the lower house of
the Dutch Parliament . . . a majority of members . . . were
in favour of giving asylum-seekers the benefit of the
doubt. Schmitz promised that no refugee families with
children would be abandoned on the streets.

*Ecumenical News International Bulletin*, 29 October 1997

---

There is so much need in the world, so many failures of
peace and justice, that one could despair. But the churches
are not called upon to solve all issues, and no single person
can be fully involved on many fronts. What is called for

is *some* action on *some* issues, disturbing the culture of contentment, companioning the poor and dispossessed without denying their own dignity, going with God into situations of distress, crisis and suffering.

# 9

# Ecumenism

Is companionship possible among the churches? The short answer to that is a resounding 'Yes', and it is demonstrated daily in ecumenical parishes, in Churches Together in Britain and Ireland and its component parts, and in countless relations and activities which would have been unthinkable fifty years ago. There are dialogues going on between radically different churches, like the one between the Catholics and the Reformed. Episcopal churches, and churches of the Reformation have less distance to cross to understand each other, and have made significant advances. But the Catholics and the Reformed found that they even narrated the history of the sixteenth and seventeenth centuries very differently, and that out of these differences had come ecclesial cultures.

> The very recognition that this is the case marks significant progress in our attempt to rid our memories of resentments and misconceptions. We need to set ourselves more diligently, however, to the task of reconciling these memories by writing together the story of what happened in the sixteenth century . . . But, above all, for the ways in which our divisions have caused a scandal, and been an obstacle to the preaching of the gospel, we need to ask forgiveness of Christ and of each other.[1]

Given that memories go to creating identities, and that in times of antagonism the memories are of opposition and rivalry, their reconciliation is no easy matter. In a thoughtful discussion of that in relation to Northern Ireland (where again the principal difficulties lie between the Reformed and the Catholics) Frank Wright concludes:

> Ecumenism must be subversive of denominational justification of national antagonism, but it would become a political tactic if it attempted to deny the fact of the national division which is a product of history. Nothing useful can be said about the division unless it is seen as a fact – a malignancy and a trap, perhaps – but a fact nonetheless.[2]

So if ecumenism is to reconcile memories it has to be without suppression or arousing Jeremiah's complaint:

> They have treated the wound of my people carelessly, saying 'Peace, peace' where there is no peace (Jer.6.14).

What that kind of consideration shows is that companionship is not like the arrival of a friendly puppy who wants to play games with an available human, but has to be something much more context- and people-sensitive. Those who offer it may have as much to learn about themselves as those to whom it is offered.

The same kind of sensitivity is in evidence as Protestants, Catholics and Orthodox work through the way in which each church has not only a foundation in faith, but also a ' "hierarchy" of truths', varying in the different cases, in relation to that foundation. The phrase comes from Vatican II (Decree on Ecumenism, 11), and 'hierarchy' here means an ordering of importance. The Joint Working Group between the Roman Catholic Church and the WCC reports some success in, first, making participants aware of how, in fact, they do rank their truths, and, second, coming to some appreciation of the values enshrined in different rankings. 'The Roman Catholic Church is finding a new appreciation of the doctrine of justification by faith' while Reformation churches 'increasingly acknowledge the significance of episcopal ministry'.[3]

This represents an advance in understanding, though not a denial of difference, made possible by walking with others who were once utterly estranged.

Yet in the early days of the WCC the hope and drive for 'visible unity' was very high on the ecumenical agenda, with division counted as sin. Much appeal was (and still is) made to Christ's prayer in John 17.21, 'that they may all be one' applied to different branches of the church. But that desired visible unity has not materialized and, in my own estimation, is unlikely, and may not even be desirable. I have two reasons for this conclusion.

The first comes from the viewpoints of the Orthodox churches and the Roman Catholic Church on intercommunion, viewpoints which are governed by their understanding of the church.

> For the Orthodox 'communion' involves a mystical and sanctifying unity created by the Body and Blood of Christ, which makes them 'one body and one blood with Christ', and therefore they can have no differences in the faith. There can be 'communion' only between local churches which have unity of faith, ministry and sacraments. For this reason the concept of 'Intercommunion' has no place in Orthodox ecclesiology.[4]

The same emphasis on oneness in faith, worship and ecclesiastical life can be found in the Roman Catholic Church as a prerequisite, except in extreme circumstances, for access to eucharistic communion.[5] For both churches, therefore, the sharing of communion will take place as a final celebration when unity is achieved, rather than being a sign of companionship on the way, as most Protestants would interpret it in relation to ecumenicity, even when a lofty view of the sacrament is held.

These official strictures do not prevent individuals from joining in the celebration of communion with members of other churches, and have also provoked some robust responses. Adrian Hastings, for instance, himself a Catholic, writes:

> Insofar as anyone, including the hierarchical authority of any church, endeavours to prevent intercommunion, its institutions should be disregarded, charitably but firmly, as unchristian, wrong, uncatholic and *ultra vires*.[6]

It may be that the official position of the churches will simply be eroded from below, but while I am aware of strong-minded Catholics sharing in Protestant communions and vice-versa, I am not aware of any similar move in relation to the Orthodox.

The difficulties of intercommunion thus form one reason for my doubt about visible unity. The other is not primarily theological, but sociological with theological implications. The WCC and many of its member churches have shared in that change of values which is part of postmodernity, with the result that diversity ceases to be something which must be overcome or rendered innocuous in the drive towards unity, and becomes instead something to be enjoyed. Hastings, again, cheerfully defends the need for difference, and gives a positive evaluation even to schism.

> Schism was not just sinful division, but was also, again and again, the rough expression of a determination on both sides to adhere to genuine truths and values of many sorts: to ensure and retain a necessary and enriching diversification of the total tradition in a way that could not apparently be achieved on any single model.[7]

Much of this book has already been celebrating diversity, but here I wish to use its existence to argue back to a form of intercommunion already available to us. The argument begins from the many and varied cultural apprehensions of God. Lamin Sanneh lists familiar Western designations such as Luther's 'mighty fortress'. He could have added the inven-

tion of the maritime British: God as Pilot. In exactly the same
way there is a plethora of images, unfamiliar to the West,
from Africa, where God may be seen as:

> the dewy-nosed One of a cattle-owning culture, the One of
> the sacred stake of a pig-herding people, the nimble-footed
> One of the sacred dance, and the long-necked One of a
> hunting group.[8]

What, then, can unite such disparate conceptions of God,
or ensure that one God is the focus of them all? Sanneh
continues:

> These differences [between Europeans and Africans, and
> among tribes] are unique and particular even though these
> *many* groups represent the *one* idea of humanity. What
> unites them, however, is more than a question of species,
> but their common *relationship* in respect to God. For this
> reason the cultural signs and symbols that *differentiate*
> them in their respective particularities *unite* them in rela-
> tion to God. It is God as this third term who thus norma-
> tively unites what cultural forms descriptively differentiate.

There may, of course, be objections to a particular rendering
of God from within the values of the faith. But Sanneh is
clear that one must not reduce all this cultural variety to 'a
warm, genial construction of the idea of "God"'.

> In this way the totality and range of human experience can
> be postulated of God's infinite manifestations, refractions
> and visitations.

'God is thus this third term who normatively unites what
cultural forms descriptively differentiate.' That understanding of God may be applied equally to our different forms
of eucharistic communion. God, present at all communions,
creates thereby an inclusive unity even among the differences

and exclusions practised by the churches. On this issue
Hastings is at one with Sanneh:

> The act of communion, each in one's own church, in fact
> establishes intercommunion and the essential sacramental
> unity of the church, whether or not we verbally recognize
> it.[9]

On that understanding of God's role visible unity and agreements among churches may still be desirable for enlarged
understanding, as witness and for co-operation, especially if
different strengths from different churches can be encom-
passed. But these are not the most basic affirmation of unity.
For with God as 'third party' in Sanneh's term, continuing
differences themselves are united, indeed unavoidably united
in the ecumenicity of God.

The problem of difference which the churches face (or
ignore) and the solution outlined here, may also be expressed
in terms of the theology which undergirds this book, in this
case specifically on the difference between God as Friend and
God as Companion. Friendship, as I have described it earlier,
is the private, intimate relationship between two people,
and God's relationship with us each privately is of the same
character. Companionship is the wider accompaniment
(God's and ours) with all that is going on.

But individual church families, or groups within them,
have behaved as if their own total relationship with God
were private friendship, unique and special to them, so that
the only way to reach this relationship was through their
own doors. All churches have behaved in this way to some
extent. But what is suitable for an individual private relationship, which by its nature excludes others, is not suitable for a
whole church with its many varied members and public face.
God *companions* the churches while *befriending* each individual. And if God is seen to companion all the churches, let
alone all of creation, exclusivity is out of place. No one may
demand that others be friends of God on their own private

terms. There are many doors, variously different, by which one may enter, without denying the effectiveness of the God-companioned others.

The German Protestants in Romania used to organize their congregations . . . with particular rules and forms for community life . . . by means of which they made sharp distinctions between themselves and those of other confessions . . . Today they can no longer do this. The . . . exodus of people, especially young people and children, means that our parishes no longer have the number to organize either celebrations or burials. And what have we found? Orthodox Romanians and Hungarian Catholics are coming to our aid: they are ready to help plan celebrations and bury the dead. They have become 'a new ecumenical neighbourhood' and are included in parish life as brothers and sisters, bringing about an openness which has never been there before. This readiness to be open crosses boundaries and clears away barriers. The fear of being taken over by those of other beliefs and those who speak other languages, and losing our identity is gradually dwindling. And the little Lutheran church in Romania is finding that with its specific gifts, it can make a distinctive contribution to the ecumenical movement and to the society around it. Ecumenism is our destiny – all of us. No church can withdraw from our globalizing world. It is the survival of all of us which is at stake.

Christoph Klein, 'Turning to God for Renewal in Mission', *International Review of Mission*, October 1998, p.479

Further, churches may companion each other, as increasingly they do, putting into practice the ecumenical adage not to do separately what can be done together. The new nomenclature 'Churches Together' witnesses to the intention for that co-operation and synergy. The advances are real. When

the ecumenical movement began it was not even clear
whether churches could pray together. Patey sees this as an
advance towards maturity:

> A church which consists of opposing factions turning deaf
> ears to one another is an immature church. A maturing
> church is one in which diversity is seen, not primarily as a
> problem to be solved, but as an opportunity to be grasped
> for reaching out to new goals of understanding and mutual
> trust. This latter path is more risky and less safe than the
> former, but it leads to a greater enrichment of life.[10]

The unity of the church may thus be understood today to
include a discerning enjoyment of diversity and an unwillingness to draw sharp lines of demarcation (or even, à la Hastings, to ignore the lines drawn by church powers). It is only
hostile confrontation which breaks the already-given unity.

But unity is not the only mark of the church affected by
the ecumenical movement. Catholicity, the mark of the
church's wholeness, has undergone a sea-change, indeed one
should say yet another sea-change. Conceptions of what
constitutes the wholeness of any church is no longer to be
measured in terms of items on a Western agenda of fullness,
but in terms of acceptance of a much wider and more varied
expression of Christian belief. 'Catholicity' was glossed by an
African group as not only belonging to the church universal,
but as having 'a respect for, and an encouragement of, the
enriching difference of culture, tradition and experience'.[11]

Konrad Raiser, the General Secretary of the WCC, spells
this out further.

> Neither a form of globalization nor a mere acquiescence in
> plurality, catholicity is based on the recognition that the
> fullness of God's presence is to be experienced in each
> local community which gathers in the name of Christ,
> which recognizes its essential and unbreakable relation-
> ship with all other such local communities. The tension

between the local church and the universal church must be transformed into a relational understanding of a world-wide church with its foundation in the local communities assembled in each place.[12]

In that case, to be catholic is to be open to the world-wide and history-long varieties of the church, to be hospitable to African and Asian versions without prejudgment.

This conception is not without its problems of what may be acceptable Christian interpretations. Some baulk at the insistence of Africans that their 'living dead' ancestors are still to be consulted within the Christian community. Some find too syncretistic the alignment of a Korean boddhisatva with the Holy Spirit, or the suggestion that the Tao may do for Chinese Christianity what the Logos did for the Greeks. Yet all versions of Christianity have taken elements from the local culture into the faith, including the pre-Christian culture of Europe.[13] The post-Enlightenment Western version is another instance of culture affecting what is believed. It will again be the case that 'by their fruits you shall know them'. It is also worth considering, in the matter of the inescapability of cultural input, the catch-22 situation of translators of the Bible. Only the word for the most high God in the culture will do to translate 'God', yet that word itself comes fraught with the overtones of the earlier religion and its culture.

Although there are difficulties, this vision of the church is one of a community of communities rather than a number of individual organizations or institutions. Konrad Raiser, accepting this view of catholicity, comments further:

> The ecumenical character of each local community is then measured by how far it is prepared to recognize its indissoluble relationship with all other communities as members of the worldwide body of Christ. This relationship is acknowledged not only in mutual support and solidarity, but also in recognizing differences and accepting mutual accountability to each other.[14]

With vernacular translation missionaries introduced a new level of complexity into Christian usage. In the multi-lingual setting of tribal societies, concepts of God reson-ated with ancient usage, with refinements taking place in incidents of ritual observance and customary practice. Often it is not the jealous god of Calvinistic clericalism that translators had adopted, or thought they were adopt-ing, for the vernacular scriptures, but the polyonomous deity of the tribe, resplendent with theophorous titles.

Lamin Sanneh, 'Theological Method in Cultural Analysis', *International Review of Mission*, Jan-April 1995, p.55

That totality of catholicity may be a long way from where some churches are now, but it can begin from where they are now. With the redefinition catholicity may no longer be used as a term of superiority by some churches who define whole-ness only in their own private terms. It is now a challenge to *all* churches, especially churches with a long and cherished tradition, to look beyond their own comfortable domesti-city and private relation with God. Hans Küng shows the contradiction inherent in those who see some feature of their own church conferring a catholicity which they deny to others:

[A]ny kind of limitation, whether spatial or numerical, temporal or social or cultural, so far from being a sign of catholicity, is more likely to be a sign of uncatholicity.[15]

But does this more open attitude mean that anything goes? It does not, for the last two traditionally-held and still potent marks of the church are holiness and apostolicity.

These marks are less concerned with ecumenical synergy as such, but they go to make up the churches which would engage in such openness. Apostolicity in this context cannot be the assumption of a smooth historical succession and the transfer of power down the ages, for that again would lock a church into its private history and cut it off from companionship. Again Küng expresses well this mark for today:

> The apostles are dead: there are no new apostles. But the *apostolic mission* remains . . . Since the apostolic mission remains, so, too, does the apostolic ministry. This apostolic ministry does not depend on further vocations to apostleship in the narrow sense, but depends on obedience to the apostles as the original witnesses and messengers of the Lord.[16]

And who are these followers of the apostles? For Küng there is only one answer: the whole church. 'We do, after all, confess an apostolic *church*.' Apostolic succession is fulfilled when the organization of a church permits it to witness to its day and culture as the apostles witnessed in theirs, and when it serves as the apostles served. There is nothing here to constrain the vision of a community of communities.

Finally, the church is holy. Holiness has often been construed as set apart in the sense of untouchable, as the ark of the covenant was untouchable on its journey to its resting place. Its power killed any who would have steadied it (IChron.13.9). Some echo of this untouchability has remained in later accounts of the church's holiness. But the difference holiness makes does not have to be understood in terms of setting apart. Certainly the church is a different kind of collection of people from others, and cannot be described without remainder in sociological terms.

But what makes the difference is not an inherent quality of the church, but the grace of God. Through God's grace the sacraments, the worship, the ministry and actions of the church may enact in their own finite and fallible way in time and space the goodness, the love, the concern for justice, the ecumenity, the specialness of God, and thus be holy. Of course the church will also fail to a greater or lesser extent to make these manifest. It is sinful as well as holy. But here too grace forgives and makes the continuation of the divine-human relationship possible.

All the marks of the church are not the church's own, but the signs of God at work in their midst. So no church may cut itself off from relationship with any other church wherever holiness and apostolicity as I have described them are present. If God is the 'third term' in all our differences, and God is ecumenical, who are we to deny fellowship?

# 10

# Mission

When I was thirteen, I was arbitrarily 'saved' by an insistent woman with her Bible open at Romans 10.9,10. Indeed I allowed myself to be saved as quickly as possible to get away from her. From that experience I developed the notion that mission was about nobbling the unsuspecting unsaved and saving them with a ready text forthwith. That view was certainly modified over time, but there was news enough of crusades and evangelical campaigns through the years to keep the basic conception alive. I was therefore taken aback to find I had been nominated to what was then called the Commission on Mission of the WCC. But that was the beginning of a steep learning curve and a whole new way of understanding what mission might be.

The greatest thing that changed was my perspective. I had thought missions were activities of the churches, or groups within them, locally or overseas. But now I discovered that the emphasis was on the *missio Dei*, God's mission. God is, in a sense, self-sent from the glory and fullness of divinity to seek and to save, 'creating the church on the way' in Moltmann's phrase.[1] Or, as David Bosch puts it: 'It is not the church which "undertakes" mission; it is the *missio Dei* which constitutes the church.'[2]

Mission, therefore, is not so much activity on behalf of God as participating in what God is already about. And when the church is truly being church it concurs with God and allies its energies with God's. Mission is not *for* God, or *in place of* God, but *with* God. This change has occurred right across the theological spectrum.

A friend in the Evangelical Foreign Missions Association recently reminded me of the new Southern Baptist slogan: 'On a mission *with* God'. He continued, 'In previous times it would have said "on a mission *for* God" . . . For the last thirty years Evangelical missions had what I have called an engineering and management mentality. If you had the right resources, motivated people and deployed them with the right tools, then World Evangelization was right around the corner.' The shift has been to the realization that it is God who brings men and women to faith. Mission *with* God meant that our proper role is to discern what God is doing in the world and co-operate with that.[3]

That represents a profound theological shift, part of the increasing emphasis on the immanence of the transcendent God within the world. Out of that divine mission, paradigmatically expressed in Jesus Christ, has come the church, which is given the privilege and responsibility of working with God as the mission continues.

[T]he *missio Dei* notion has helped to articulate the conviction that neither the church nor any other human agent can ever be considered the author or bearer of mission. Mission is, primarily and ultimately, the work of the triune God, Creator, Redeemer and Sanctifier, for the sake of the world, a ministry in which the church is privileged to participate. Mission has its origin in the heart of God. God is a fountain of sending love. This is the deepest source of mission. It is impossible to penetrate deeper still; there is mission because God loves people.[4]

'There is mission because God loves people.' In the terms I have used in this book God already has a relationship from the divine side with everyone – again because God loves people. Churches are called on to embody and enact that truth – thereby putting their energies with God's.

If mission is God's the first requirement of the church is

that it should work with God. Finding God at work, however, is not a matter of geographical survey, nor statistical analysis of congregations and outsiders. For in the end there is nowhere where God is not, nowhere is heathen, nowhere is secular in the sense of God being absent, and it is always a possibility, everywhere for everyone, that the saving, confronting, forgiving, energizing presence of God may be encountered and life transformed. So going with God in the final analysis is going *as God goes*, wherever that might be. In other words, since God is, in the full sense, *with* others, the second requirement of mission/evangelism/outreach is to share that quality of 'withness'. Mission is not *to* people *for* God, but *with* God *with* people.

That second requirement rules out the kind of experience with which I began this chapter, and which still continues. Many still pursue the rapid saving of souls, believing that some kind of affirmation of faith, an assent to preferred doctrine, however little understood, or attendance at the Church of the Evangelist, represents salvation and may be counted a success. At the moment Russia is flooded with such eager fishers, as if Christianity had not existed there for over a thousand years. And, unlike the Russian Orthodox Church, these evangelists have money to spend.

> Groups that come in from the outside have the money to do what they want to do, whether that is to lease halls, buy television time etc. For instance, a Swedish group – the 'Word of Life' mission – has established groups right across the north-east of Russia. They publish their own newspaper. The headline across the front page of one of these was 'God give us Russia'.[5]

But it is not only mission from the rich North Atlantic countries which can behave in this imperialist fashion. Some Korean churches are also intensely evangelistic in other countries, disregarding local churches for the honour of their own.

The Korean missionary personnel are put on fast track job contracts. They enter the country with little or no orientation, with hardly a word of the local language and are expected to give honour to the sending church in a period of three to five years. Furthermore, all honour must be measurable and quantifiable, and to be honour at all it must – in the clearest of terms – be the work of the sending church. It is this situation that forces Korean missionary personnel to do what they do, and becomes an obstacle to meaningful relationship in partnership.[6]

Not all Korean churches are in that mould, just as not all evangelical outreach is so sweeping. Further, British churches in the past have sent people out equally imperialistically, and, in relation to honour, Anglicans, Lutherans, Presbyterians, Methodists and others who once planted churches of their own kind overseas, leading to the honour of the originating church and its family, are hardly in a position to cast the first stone. What is important out of this survey is not the inherent criticism, but its foundation, encapsulated in a Korean's comment deploring his compatriots' zeal: 'Their missionary thinking is quite unyielding, for they regard people of other faiths [indeed of other churches] as objects to be evangelized.'[7]

'Objects to be evangelized': that really says it all about this form of mission. These are not *people* to be cared about and loved, let alone people whom God loves. Nor are they seen to be people in their own context – their culture, their social conditions, a faith which matters to them (including the Christian faith for 'sheep stealing' is common). Rather they are convenient targets for the evangelist. The important thing is evangelism and its 'success', while people exist only to further the evangelist's opportunities for success. This is light years away from Bosch's description of God as a fountain of sending love.

Augustine, faced with Donatist heretics, may have felt justified in recommending compulsion for their return to the

There is a story concerning a meeting between Bertrand Russell and a missionary home from China. 'Tell me,' he said, 'do you believe that all those who have never heard of Christ will be damned?'

'No,' said the missionary, 'not if they have never heard. But if they have heard and rejected him, then they are lost.'

'Well,' Russell replied, 'how many have you preached to?'

'Oh, about ten thousand'

'And of these how many became Christian?'

'Around thirty.'

'In that case, on your own showing, you are personally responsible for 9970 souls being condemned to hell!'

church, but there is no such pressure visible in Jesus' ministry which might support an aggressive campaign. Instead Jesus made himself available to all and sundry, incarnating the open accessibility of God. Jesus enacted paradigmatically in himself and in what he did the concurrence and synergy of the human and the divine. He saw a similar synergy happening in other people: 'Your faith has made you whole.' But nowhere is there pressure. Instead there is the thereness of Jesus, the attraction of his words and actions, and implicit therein an offer which may evoke a response.

From the Syro-Phoenician woman Jesus learned that such response could extend beyond the boundaries of 'the house of Israel' (Matt.15.24). Paul's missionary understanding took him even further, describing Jesus as the one who broke down the walls of separation between Jew and Gentile, making peace between them (Eph.2.14). But instead of using Pauline conceptions of the peace Jesus brings about, the Christian church in mission has often preferred to extrapolate from his image of a Christian soldier: 'Soldiers of Christ, arise'; we are 'marching as to war'; 'Who is on the Lord's side, who will fight the foe?' And war may be conducted only by deliberately

forgetting the humanity of the enemy. Leonardo Boff describes the full fury of this metaphor in action in the church's
attitude to the natives of Latin America. Other later missionaries may have been less military, but the underlying attitudes
often remained.

> The native Indian was an infidel to be fought and subdued.
> Mission work was a holy war. Instead of real human
> encounter, the Constantinian system of Christian Europe
> was imposed by fire and sword. No serious theological
> approach to the religions of the native civilizations was
> made. They were viewed as the work of the Devil, to be
> exorcized and extinguished. All too often the Indians were
> viewed as something less than human, as irrational and
> beastly creatures.[8]

But, in defence of traditional mission, it may be argued
that Jesus sent out his own disciples on a missionary enterprise, equipped only with the good news, even telling them to
shake the dust off their feet from places unwilling to hear
them. John Oman once called such an action 'the forgotten
sacrament', for it is an action prescribed by Jesus, but one
which the church no longer practises.[9] But although Oman
was writing in the 1920s, long before thoughts of the mission
of God, his analyses would not give comfort to pressing
preachers, since he never forgets God's role in the whole
process.

> The human agent lays down his task, but he does not
> merely abandon it. He leaves it with God, knowing that
> God will take it up again, in judgment, it may be, but in a
> judgment directed by love. With the close of opportunity
> man's task lies elsewhere, but God has other occasions and
> other messengers.[10]

The difference with Oman is that he does not believe that
people may be bludgeoned or cajoled or pressed into believ-

ing. Only love will find a way to elicit response from the freedom of the other. If love is rejected, then that has to be accepted.

> God has made in every heart a sanctuary into which only the persuasion of love has a right to enter, a sanctuary into which he himself will not, with any other means, force an entrance. In view of this great fact the church should learn from her Lord how to fail, not in discouragement, much less in indifference, but in faith, hope and love.[11]

Doubts about impersonal or pressurizing missionary methods do not imply that the Christian faith may never be proclaimed. Rather they are directed towards the perception that the *method* of proclamation must cohere with its *content*, which is God with us in its aspects of relationship, reconciliation and transformation. In McLuhan's still valid analysis, 'the medium is the message'. If the medium shows no love, no concern, no being-with those addressed, why believe the message?

This, indeed, is where mission anywhere in terms of word/message, and mission in terms of solidarity on matters of peace and justice, meet. The one can hardly do without the other. 'With' is the deciding term. On the one hand, only if people are *with* those they are addressing, and on the other hand only if the recipients know the reasons of faith for the solidarity, is there genuine mission which has both something to say and which does not make objects of its hearers. A Baptist mission in one of Costa Rica's shanty towns shows how even traditional evangelical processes may change.

> We began in the streets with the boys and girls, asking permission of their parents to share God's Word with them. We prayed, played games, shared some food we had prepared ... We persevered in faith, humbly, steadfastly, and in awareness of the reality around us. We adopted Christ's own model of evangelization – going to where the

crowd was. This process had a great impact on our lives. We realized that the traditional model of evangelism was not suited to this context, for the content of the message must bring hope, not condemnation. We had to learn with the people – to feel the way that they feel, speaking to them in their own language.[12]

So mission with God and with people demands in the first place accepting them as they are where they are in all their present diversity. That is something the church has to relearn constantly, whether it is a bourgeois church in relation to the poor, or a Western church in relation to the South. In what follows I shall be considering what were once called 'foreign missions', but the implications are often the same for the 'home' variety.

Missions, whether home or overseas, flourished in the nineteenth and twentieth centuries, just when modernity was at its height, with its one model of how things should be. Understandably missionaries imbued with such consciousness took it with them when they went overseas. Therefore, for all their undoubted desire to serve Christ, their good work and self-giving, unfortunate characteristics of modernity made themselves felt. At the time it appeared to church people that God had especially favoured the Christian West, in everything from democracy to education, science, health and the standard of living. Missionaries, therefore, thought of themselves as bringing these benefits to those without them along with the gospel. But at the same time that implied that they went as the favoured to the unfavoured, the enlightened to the unenlightened, the successful to the unsuccessful, the civilized to the uncivilized, as well as the Christian to the 'heathen'. As a result there are positive and negative results of past mission. Positively, as seen in 1968, and in addition to preaching the gospel:

[t]he missionary movement made a prime contribution to the abolition of slavery; spread better methods of agri-

culture; established and maintained unnumbered schools; gave medical care to millions; elevated the status of women; created bonds between people of different countries ... trained a significant segment of the nations now newly independent.[13]

Negatively, however:

The problem was that the advocates of mission were blind to their own ethnocentrism. They confused their middle-class ideals and values with the tenets of Christianity. Their views about morality, respectability, order, efficiency, individualism, professionalism, work and technical progress, having been baptized long before, were without compunction exported to the ends of the earth. They were, therefore, predisposed not to appreciate the cultures of the people to whom they went – the unity of living and learning; the interdependence between individual, community, culture and industry; the profundity of folk wisdom; the proprieties of traditional societies – all these were swept aside by a mentality shaped by the Enlightenment which tended to turn people into objects, reshaping the entire world into the image of the West, separating humans from nature and one another, and 'developing' them according to Western standards and suppositions.[14]

What that shows, at best, is an attitude of benevolent paternalism ('daughter churches') and at worst authoritarian diktat. It is worth stressing that point repeatedly, for its results are deeply resented by the churches in virtually all the countries to which missionaries were sent. J. N. K. Mugambi, of the University of Nairobi, is typical:

[T]he modern missionary enterprise has presupposed that the African culture and religious heritage is an unsuitable rootstock on which to graft the gospel. Thus the African has been considered a cultural blank on which anything could be written. Hence the competition among many missionary agencies for the African soul.[15]

The result, Mugambi writes, is that Christianity has become a 'Sunday religion', with the rest of the week being traditional African 'business as usual'.

> Perhaps this is one way of explaining the fact that countries which boast a majority of membership to Christian denominations could suffer as much devastation as Rwanda did in 1994.[16]

Rwanda was ninety per cent Christian, and Mugambi suggests that its conflict indicates 'that at the cultural level the missionary enterprise has not entered the African psyche'. For Africans Christianity remains 'an appendix to their cultural and religious identity'. To the extent that that is true it shows that for Africans – as for Indians, British and all the rest – unless Christianity is expressed in the local culture it will not take deep roots. Where it is taking deeper roots now is, perhaps, in the independent African Instituted Churches which blend Christianity with African beliefs and practices, and also in the greater cultural freedom practised by the 'mainline' churches now.

This acknowledgment of the role local culture plays does not imply the endorsement of any culture in its totality, but it

---

The gospel cannot be completely adjusted, indigenized, contextualized, accommodated, adapted, resymbolized, acculturated, inculturated and incarnated to culture. The gospel displays its authentic power in its refusal to be completely indigenized . . . A perfect indigenization is an idolatry of culture.

K. Koyama, 'The Tradition and Indigenization', *Asia Journal of Theology*, April 1993, p.7

does imply that gestures are not enough: 'It is not enough to replace the gothic chasuble with an indigo loincloth.'[17] To see how religion and culture in fact interact Claude Geffré looked again at 'the hellenization of Christianity' – the encounter between the Christian religion in its first centuries and the Greek culture of the time. He finds the phrase only partially true. 'One could also rightly speak of the Christianization of Hellenism.' The involvement was:

more than an adaptation to the language and patterns of thought of the dominant culture. It involves rather the metamorphosis of the conceptual resources and existing values into a new synthesis in which the Christian message is the catalysing factor.[18]

That work towards a new synthesis is going on in many places where formerly the Western pattern was introduced, and companionship here on the part of British churches is to allow that to happen with encouragement but without interference, and to accept the diversity of Christianity which will result. But the quest for a new synthesis is equally the task of churches in Britain today, faced with a largely post-modern society when the roots of their present form lies in modernity. Geffré poses a searching question:

Is the gospel rejected simply because it is the Word of God, challenging human situations, or because it is tied to a historical past which is already passé? . . . Does [the word of the witness] promote a new existence of this or that man or woman based on the fundamental experiences through which they interpret their own lives?[19]

These are large and inescapable questions which have to be faced in each particular context. But a more practical matter which may be considered here is the kind of relationship between the mainline churches in Britain and those countries in which this reorientation is proceeding. Most have moved some way from the former paternalism, at least to think in terms of partnership. 'Partnership' is a good word to use here. It has the values of companionship – being-with, walking-with, supporting and encouraging each other – but also connotes working together towards a common end, no matter how different the partners may be. What the churches have to avoid in this situation is the temptation to be the dominant partner with the available finance, and dictate what is to happen through financial control.

---

### Aid out of Africa for Aberdeen's needy

The poor of Aberdeen, the affluent oil capital of Europe, have been sent generous support . . . A charitable organization in Bulawayo, Aberdeen's twin city in Zimbabwe, which has often benefited from the Scots' generosity, has sent the Lord Provost a £50 cheque to show its concern for the needy of the north-east . . . Dignitas, a group offering advice and training to the unemployed . . . wants to promote the concept of 'reverse aid'. They are keen to highlight how developing countries do not want to feel that they are always on the receiving end of charity but can make their own contributions. While £50 may not seem much . . . it would be more than four years' earnings. Unemployment, at 1.8% in Aberdeen, is 18% in Bulawayo, where at least 40% of the population is thought to be HIV positive.

Graeme Smith, *The (Glasgow) Herald*, 17 February 1999

---

What this equality in the faith means in practice may be neatly demonstrated by the Anglican Communion's ten 'Principles of Partnership' which I give briefly here. Again, while the intended reference of these principles is world-wide relations among Anglicans the principles could well be applied with considerable challenge among different church families in Britain, where the devolution of power is much less in evidence, or among local church communities.

1. *Local Initiative:* the responsibility for mission belongs to the church in that place.

2. *Mutuality:* open and joint accountability; sharing power.

3. *Responsible stewardship:* resources jointly owned and held in trust for the common good.

4. *Interdependence:* no absolute donors or absolute recipients. '[W]e are incomplete and cannot be called the Church of God if the diversity implicit in our catholicity is overtaken by a parochial, cultural or racial homogeneity.'

5. *Cross-fertilization:* a willingness to learn from one another.

6. *Integrity:* all partners are essentially equal; a commitment to be real and honest.

7. *Transparency:* openness and honesty; taking the risk of being hurt, misunderstood and taken advantage of.

8. *Solidarity:* commitment to one another in Christ's body; no one to be left to suffer alone.

9. *Meeting together:* for evaluation, self-assessment and cross-cultural fertilization.

10. *Acting ecumenically:* exploring ways of being involved in mission co-operatively with other Christians.[20]

In conclusion, then, all mission is God's mission arising from God's love. It is the impact of God's gracious presence with its offer of relationship everywhere. Mission does not belong to the churches, but they may have the excitement and privilege of being caught up in the *missio Dei*. To participate in mission is to work as God works, not as if the gospel were a packaged commodity to be exported to its recipient objects, but with the gospel as liberating and transforming good news of God and Christ within a particular context, good news which is to be lived out as well as preached within that context. Numbers of converts are not the criteria of evangelistic success. Rather, true mission is happening wherever and whenever the unconditional love, the intimate friendship and the invigorating companionship of God is made known to others by those who have experienced it.

# 11

# Other Faiths

'Other faiths' used to connote strange beliefs and practices from distant lands of which the British knew little. Today, however, schoolchildren learn the rudiments of many faiths, each taught as a religion in its own right. Further, with the arrival of so many people of other faiths in Britain since the 1960s, so that now they may be found from the corner shop to the House of Commons, contact and friendship with them becomes a more ordinary experience. And, although racism and intolerance undoubtedly exist in Britain, I believe John Hick to be on the whole right when he gives a positive spin to this coexistence:

> For many people it has become an assumption of daily life that our Jewish or Muslim or Hindu or Sikh or Buddhist friends and acquaintances are as fully entitled, in the sight of God, to live by their own religious traditions as we are to live by ours.[1]

But does this *de facto* acceptance of pluralism imply that the churches should follow the same route? I shall argue that while acceptance of pluralism may be part of the churches' response, that cannot be arrived at by simple indifference ('live and let live' on its own), for that would leave a great theological lacuna between themselves and the other faiths practised here now. It would also deprive the churches of opportunities for gaining new perspectives on themselves and the world.

For the necessary theology, the contrast is once more

between a past when God was held to be primarily transcendent, and a present when the immanence of God is taken with much greater seriousness. When God was thought of as transcendent, dwelling distantly in heaven, it was possible to think that divine self-revelation could be directed towards one place but not another (to Israel, for instance, but not to China), although that belief in the specificity of revelation always sat oddly with belief that God created the whole world, and was a God of love. The consequence was that those areas in which it was believed that there was no divine revelation could be described as dark, ungodly, unreached, and the missionary call was to 'take' God and Christ there, in a somewhat similar way as one might 'take' British trade, or ideas of democracy.

But if, instead of this occasional and partial presence, God's omnipresence and offer of relation to all is fully appreciated, the perception changes. Nowhere is simply ungodly; an omnipresent God cannot be taken anywhere, for God is there and everywhere already. Many Christian missionaries arrived at the same conclusion from their experience overseas. Richard Drummond, an American Presbyterian who went to Japan, records this change in his own thinking and has found it in many others.

> This openness to surprise, surprise that the finest qualities of Christic [Christlike] faith and obedience can be found in what some might call unexpected persons and places has characterized the most sensitive Christian missionaries of every age, from Gregory Thaumaturgos to Matteo Ricci, from Francis Xavier to Christian Friedrich Schwartz, from Nicholas von Zinzendorf to Guido Verbeck.[2]

From the perspective of belief in an omnipresent God, a God who may be taken to different places looks like a tribal god in competition with other local gods, rather than the Maker of heaven and earth, in the credal affirmation. But if God is omnipresent, always in relation and seeking response, then that response is everywhere possible and indeed will have occurred in many places, so the appearance of Christ-like qualities becomes less of a surprise.

The results of such response to divine presence, or, in Hick's term which includes the non-theistic Buddhists, response to the Real, are understandably varied partly on account of the individuality of humans, partly because all human responses to God or the Real are largely shaped by the culture from which they emerge – the language, the concepts and the values of that culture, although the experience will also lead to critiques of that culture. Acceptance of the world's faiths as various, and variously elaborated, responses to the presence of God is assisted if it is also believed that God enjoys diversity – and indeed, if God does not, creation must be a continuous disappointment.

The belief that unity, in terms of a singleness of faith, expresses the will of God, appears much less compelling than once it did. That belief looks now like a reflection of modernity's drive to make everything over in its own image. And the diatribes that were once hurled against non-Christian faiths – often out of ignorance of their actuality – now seem harsh and blinkered. The undoubtedly Christian and missionary-minded David Bosch can write:

> We do not have [God] in our pocket, so to speak, and do not just 'take him' to the others; he accompanies us and also comes towards us ... We are all recipients of the same mercy, sharing in the same mystery. We thus approach every other faith and its adherents reverently, taking off our shoes, as the place we are approaching is holy.[3]

Are all faiths and belief systems, then, holy? Hick offers an empirical criterion for distinguishing between faiths and movements which derive from the grace of God and those which do not, and he instances some of the more pernicious cults of recent times. In effect he is using as criterial evidence the list of the fruit of the Spirit in Galatians (5.22): Love, joy, peace, patience, kindness, generosity, faithfulness, gentleness and self-control. Where there are some people in other faiths and movements who exhibit qualities like these, qualities which arise from synergy with God, then that faith system is an 'effective context of salvific transformation'.[4] Keith Ward is also impressed by the quest for values in the different faiths:

> It might be better to see the different faiths, not as in radical opposition, but as having a range of agreed values, but varying ways of interpreting them in the light of a developing understanding of the world. There is an important sense in which differing faiths are engaged in a common pursuit of supreme value, though they conceive this in different ways.[5]

Not every member of every faith will bear the fruit or demonstrate the value, just as not every Christian does. And it may be slow growing in any faith. But where a movement produces some 'saints' of this kind it may be perceived to be a context in which God's grace can take visible form. That, however, should not be held to imply that one has to be part of a faith or movement before God's grace is encountered, for that grace is freely available to everyone everywhere, and there are saints who belong to no organization.

The people I regard as saints are strikingly unconcerned about themselves and are concerned instead to serve God, or to live out the Dharma, or the Tao, or to realize the universal Buddha nature, and we see in their lives an unselfish love and compassion that we all recognize as intrinsically valuable, indeed often awe-inspiringly so.

John Hick, *The Rainbow of Faiths*, SCM Press 1995, p.77

Hick's empirical criterion was to some extent fore-shadowed by the documents of Vatican II which were already pointing to the undoubted holiness to be found in other religions. The Declaration on the Relation of the Church to Non-Christian Religions (*Nostra Aetate*) declared 'esteem' for Islam and described what was seen as religiously significant in other faiths.

> Thus in Hinduism men contemplate the divine mystery and express it through an unspent fruitfulness of myths and through searching philosophical enquiry. They seek release from the anguish of our condition through ascetical practices or deep meditation or a loving, trusting flight towards God.

As a result prudent and loving dialogue with all was recommended.[6]

This is an eirenic and gracious Declaration, but some of the thinking behind it, particularly from Karl Rahner, has caused concern for, and among, those of other faiths. What is involved is a reference to Christ. One may speak in general of God – or of the Real. But to make mention of Christ particularizes Christianity, and when God's grace is interpreted in terms of Christ's presence in other faiths, these faiths infer that they are being subsumed once more under a Christian imperialism, especially when Rahner suggested that through God's grace they were 'anonymous Christians'.

Rahner, however, may be judged too harshly on this count. Küng argued forcefully that this was an endeavour to bring all people of good life and good will into the Roman Catholic Church by the back door, while people of other faiths knew only too well that they were 'unanonymous' in their own faith.[7] And Bosch is correct in one sense to write:

> [Rahner] never abandons the idea of Christianity as the absolute religion and of salvation having to come through

Christ. But he recognizes supernatural elements of grace in other religions which, he posits, have been given to human beings through Christ. There is saving grace within other religions, but this grace is Christ's.[8]

Yet Rahner's achievement should be recognized also. He wrote of no boundaries and no fixed points for the freedom of God's grace, breaking thereby the neo-scholastic mould which would contain it. Certainly he was writing in the christocentric 1960s, when all grace, even in relation to other faiths, was seen as coming from Christ, but he was also capable of writing:

There are impulses of grace which precede the acceptance of justification in free faith and love. And there is grace outside the Church and her sacraments.

And again, in my favourite quotation on grace anywhere:

Just because grace is *free and unmerited* this does not mean that it is rare (theology had been led astray for too long already by the tacit assumption that grace would no longer be grace if God became too free with it).[9]

What may be said of Rahner is that he loosened up Catholic and some Protestant thinking on grace, so that further advances could be made after his time.

Before considering finally where Christ comes in relation to other faiths – and how could Christianity drop that reference? – it is worth giving a more extended example. The Middle Eastern Oriental Orthodox Georges Khodr exemplifies the extrapolation of the Orthodox emphasis on the resurrection setting Christ free in all the world.

Christ is hidden everywhere in the mystery of his lowliness. Any reading of religions is a reading of Christ. It is Christ alone who is received as a light when grace visits a

Brahmin, a Buddhist or a Mohammedan reading his own scriptures. Every martyr for the truth, every man persecuted for what he believes to be right, dies in communion with Christ.[10]

Rahner and Khodr in their different ways do raise a real question for interfaith relations on the part of Christians who have found in Christ the effective revelation of God. But it is a relevant question what 'Christ' means when used as the source of all grace everywhere. This cannot refer to the specificity of Jesus of Nazareth, a man of a particular time and place. Rather it must be the cosmic Christ, whose activity in this respect is the same as that ascribed to the Holy Spirit. And since it has always been held that the effective external work of the Trinity is the action of all three together, we are back with a notion of God, though a Christian perception of that.

No doubt when Muslims join in interfaith dialogue their use of Allah is similarly particularly coloured. There is a limit to the amount of self-transcendence possible, or even desirable in a dialogue, so that, when a Christian says: 'All faiths are responses to God's presence,' the connotations of God for the speaker will be those arrived at through the Christian faith, in which Christ is central. That, however, need not lead to either a sense that no other faith has anything to contribute to dialogue, not to a sense of superiority over other faiths. After all, *all* responses, including the Christian one, are *human* responses to the ineffable God.

But does that simply relativize the Christian faith among the others? Here I must return to what was argued in Part One about the importance of relative relativism. Too many still believe that either there is a single objective truth or else all is mere opinion. But relative relativism acknowledges that my perceptions and beliefs will relate to (be relative to) my upbringing, rationality, culture, religion and so forth. That does not mean that I hold them lightly as easily-changed opinions, for they interpret and guide my life. I may give an account of them and reasons for them, and may persuade others. But I cannot think that everyone, everywhere, will be persuaded to think exactly as I do.

Even when there was thought to be objective truth (which would have to be singular and timeless) there were various schools of thought with different and therefore competing accounts of what it was. Only by an imperialism of definition, or a pragmatism over what 'worked' could anyone claim a single truth – and the power that went with it. Relative relativism is, in a sense, a recognition of that state of affairs.

Relative relativism, then, allows for both the acknowledgment of difference and the possibility of persuasion – that power of attractiveness rather than force. Relative relativism allows both for Buddhist belief from where they stand that there is no God, and my belief from where I stand that there is a God who has not been absent from Asia. Each may give reasons from within their traditions. But I may not portray Buddhists as theists. There have been some unfortunate approaches to Buddhism which inform them that 'really' there is a transcendent 'somewhat' in nirvana and their eschatological hope, so they are theists after all, though they did not recognize it. That plays the superiority game once more. On the other hand Christianity cannot be subsumed under anything else either. So it always remains possible for Christians to follow Christ, to live out the Christian life attractively and give reasons for what they believe and do when approached by enquirers or in dialogue with others.

Thus the recognition of other faiths in no way implies that the Christian faith cannot be commended. This chapter, after all, follows one on mission. But, as was emphasized earlier, 'commending' the faith is very different from trying to impose it. God-with-us draws by the power of attraction rather than ruling us by a forceful exercise of power. So commending faith in that God, whose freedom and love Christians see incarnated in Jesus Christ, will be in the attractiveness of what Christians say or do, drawing others to explore the faith, rather than in pressurizing for conversion.

The Sri Lankan theologian Wesley Ariarajah, who has seen the harm campaigns have done in his country – in, for instance, making Christianity seem like a very *foreign* religion, and disrupting local relations among the faiths – describes the way the Christian faith comes over, not as an attraction but as a threat to non-Christians, for the aim is to overpower and displace the faith of others. He quotes (without attribution): 'Two thousand years of Christian love is enough to make anybody nervous.' But, he continues, if Christ is our window on to God and the God seen through that window is one of love, then to 'say . . . that God will not love you unless you repent, or that God will not save you unless you believe in what God has done in Jesus Christ, is to reverse the order of the gospel message'.[11]

Ariarajah's conclusion is in keeping with the viewpoint of relative relativism:

> If Christians also believe that the Christ-event has a salvific significance for the whole of humanity it has to be witnessed to as a claim of faith. We cannot use this faith-claim as a basis to deny other claims of faith. However true our own experience, however convinced we are about a faith-claim, it has to be given as a claim of faith, and not as truth in the absolute sense.[12]

When that understanding has been reached it then becomes possible to dialogue with people of other faiths in order to see how the presence of God (or the Real) is expressed in their beliefs and practices, and to hear from these others how Christianity comes over to them. Dialogue does not involve a relinquishing, nor even a holding in abeyance, of the Christian faith, though it does involve serious listening. More strongly, dialogue requires commitment to the Christian faith:

We must begin with the affirmation that dialogue does
not exclude witness. In fact, when people have no convictions to share, there can be no real dialogue ... In any
genuine dialogue authentic witness must take place, for
partners will bear witness to why they have this or that
conviction.[13]

---

Apparently, even in this day and age, it takes time for the
essentially dialogical nature of the Christian faith to sink
in and take root. The evolution of themes in a series of
WCC consultations may illustrate my point. The ...
Mexico City conference (1963) used the formulation 'The
*Witness* of Christians to Men of Other Faiths'. A year later
at a ... meeting in Bangkok the theme was 'The Christian
*Encounter* with Men of Other Faiths'. Three years later, in
Sri Lanka, the word 'dialogue' surfaced; now the theme
was 'Christians in *Dialogue* with Men of Other Faiths'.
Throughout, the major participants were still identified as
*Christians* who dialogue *about* or *with* others. Only in
Ajaltoun (Lebanon) in 1970 was the mutuality of dialogue
recognized; the theme was 'Dialogue *between* Men of
Living Faiths' (the women were apparently still outside the
dialoguers' field of vision!). In 1977, then, in Chiang Mai
(Thailand) the subject was 'Dialogue in Community'.

David Bosch, *Transforming Mission*,
Orbis Books 1991, p.484

---

But both the white South African David Bosch and the Sri
Lankan Wesley Ariarajah emphasize that while commitment
to one's faith is firm, the attitude in the process of dialogue is
one of humility. As Ariarajah writes:

Even the most convinced Christian can only witness in
humility and in terms of his or her convictions, for truth is
beyond the grasp of any human being.[14]

Such humility, as Bosch comments, should be for Christians a matter of course, since the Christian faith is a religion of grace which is freely received. Further, humility must not be abused:

> The point of our humility and our repentance is not to indulge masochistically in a bout of self-flagellation, or to use our penitence as a new lever to manipulate others . . . True repentance and humility are cleansing experiences which lead to renewal and renewed commitment.[15]

In the process of dialogue the Christian is aiming neither to convert nor to be converted, but to discover from others the religious impulses and structures which shape their religion. In the process new light may be shed on Christian belief and practice. Some aspects of other faiths may not appeal; some may seem quite similar to Christianity. Some, however, may appear especially attractive and well worth considering within a Christian framework. Dialogue may be about mutual understanding, but given the belief that other faiths may be, in Hick's useful phrase, 'contexts of salvific transformation', even to someone steeped in one religion insights from another may resonate.

Two examples of such insights, one more theological, the other more practical, will point to what is possible. John Hick records the value of years of dialogue with Buddhists of the Zen and Tibetan traditions, including the attraction of 'Tibetan forms of meditation in a noticeable degree of detachment from self-concern and a flowering of serenity and kindness'.

> This encounter with Buddhism is affecting the way in which a number of leading American theologians are doing their work. None has become a Buddhist, but I think all have been impressed by Buddhist insights and values and by their embodiment in a number of Buddhists . . . [T]here can be no doubt that intellectually serious and

personally friendly sharing and comparing of ideas, histories and experiences, even between people of traditions which are theoretically as different as Christianity and Buddhism – one being theistic, the other non-theistic – can be extremely valuable.[16]

More briefly, and on a practical note, Claude Geffré of the Institut Catholique de Paris notes what other religions may offer to Christians on the way we live now:

A better knowledge of the religious traditions of the east can teach an excessively activist and overly pragmatic Christianity to rediscover the value of gratuitousness, of silence, of not being in command, of moderation in using the earth's resources.[17]

Such insights will come to Christianity only if it can bring itself in humility to be with other movements of faith. 'With' remains the defining term of the relation. To be with another is to be alongside, but, crucially, 'with' preserves a space so that neither is absorbed into the other. That is important in the relation with God: God remains God and we remain ourselves, but a relationship is offered and accepted. In the matter of dialogue with other faiths they remain themselves in their different worlds and Christianity remains itself. But a relationship of discovery and possible mutual enrichment may ensue.

Other faiths, then, need not frighten the churches, such that they withdraw from any contact with them, behaving as if they did not exist on these shores, nor need they be represented as harvest fields ready for conversion. Instead they are elaborated responses to what lies beyond all human expression – often imperfectly practised, as is Christianity, but capable of producing saints – and this becomes a further avenue of exploration of what, for Christian theists, the God who was in Christ has been doing in the world.

Thus far I have been discussing dialogue among the faiths

as if it were entirely on matters of belief. But such dialogue could have a much wider global and practical impact than that. Two of the burning issues of our time are those of peace and the ecological crisis. In both cases a combined input from the faiths might be able to make a difference. A cry comes from the Ecumenical Association of Third World Theologians that co-operation to alleviate suffering may be as important as interfaith dialogue:

[The] third world is torn apart by religious conflicts of unparalleled violence, as religious fundamentalism of every kind (Hindu, Christian, Buddhist and Muslim) intensifies, provoking sharp hostilities which provide a cover for other forms of social conflict to surface. Without a conscious concern for the liberation of the oppressed, religions in the Third World, it would seem, easily become supportive ideologies which legitimize oppression or sectarian creeds which promote divisiveness and prevent the solidarity of the oppressed.[18]

---

### Interfaith Work for Health

A courageous example of co-operation between religions is the interfaith initiative set up in 1997 in Zambia . . . [which] comprises the Christian Council of Zambia, the Episcopal councils, Evangelicals, Bahai and Muslim representatives. The interfaith initiative decided to put aside doctrinal differences and promote alternative strategies to prevent AIDS – abstinence and condoms (especially for married couples when one partner is HIV positive) . . . [They have developed] a wholistic approach to health, which includes learning about nutrition, clean water and caring for the whole person.

*Contact*, WCC, Jan–April 1999

Certainly there is a limit to what British churches can do here. John Esposito considers 'a disenchantment with, and at times a rejection of, the West' to be one of the factors fuelling Islamic revivalism.[19] Nevertheless, if it could be known that in Britain Christians and Muslims had overcome their suspicion of each other sufficiently to be talking peaceably together without compromising their religious identity, and may co-operate on issues of joint concern, that would be a kind of beacon for future possibilities elsewhere. As Alan Race argues, the faiths

> have a positive contribution to make towards the natural, ethnic and cultural interdependence that is now necessary to develop for the sake of both survival and future well-being.[20]

An instance of the 'positive contribution' was perceived by the Worldwide Fund for Nature (WWF) when in 1986 it called leaders of most faiths together in Assisi to declare the status of the natural world as divine creation, and commit themselves to its preservation. The implication was that, even though religions might differ considerably, care for non-human creation appeared in each, and it was time for the devout of all religions to apply this belief in the face of environmental degradation and spoliation. For the WWF religions offered the fastest way to reach the greatest number of ordinary people.

Martin Palmer, one of the organizers of the Assisi meeting, describes it thus:

> [F]or the first time ever environmental groups sat down with leaders of all the major faiths and with indigenous faiths, and tried to see what they could learn from one another about how to care for the earth. Since then tens of thousands of religious communities, drawing upon their own teachings and the information made available by environmental scientists, have launched their own environ-

mental programmes. The process has not left a single faith untouched, for all of them had failed to live up to or to explore their own teachings on the environment.[21]

The network set up to follow through from this meeting now has 90,000 religious communities involved 'in environmental programmes ranging from reforesting the sacred forests of Krishna in India to developing environmental Sunday School schemes for all the mainline churches of Kenya'.[22] Perhaps as well as 'Churches Together', we may develop 'Faiths Together' which would be salutary for every problematic area.

I have traced here a kind of ripple effect, from simply getting on with people of other faiths, to talking openly with them in dialogue, to working with them in the light of the problems we all face. None of this will diminish Christian identity; rather it will give it a fullness it has not had before.

---

Eternal God, whose image lies in the hearts of all people,
We live among peoples
    whose ways are different from ours,
    whose faiths are foreign to us,
    whose tongues are unintelligible to us.
Help us to remember
that you love all people with your great love,
that all religion is an attempt to respond to you,
that the yearnings of other hearts
    are much like our own
    and are known to you.
Help us to recognize you in the words of truth
    the things of beauty,
    the actions of love about us.
We pray through Christ,
who is a stranger to no one land more than to another,
and to every land no less than to another.

*Spirit, Gospel, Cultures*, WCC Publications 1995, p.31

# 12

# The Environment

There is a sense in which this book has traced a paradox of sorts: that the immanence of God elicits transcendence from human beings. The transcendence in this case is not vertical but horizontal, lateral. That is to say that because God is present everywhere in the world and the divine energies run through it all, Christians may not put up in advance protective walls round the locus of their energies in church, in society, with other churches or other faiths. Rather by transcendence of what is currently accepted they may discover God in ever widening circles. What may be new, or unknown to us is neither new nor unknown to God. And if God may not be corralled within 'us and them' divisions, neither may the churches be.

It still takes faith and courage to venture towards otherness, past the known, the tried and tested, the way things currently are. And mistakes are always possible. But the persuasion of God may be for the churches to transcend the divisions created by perceived otherness, not by annihilating them – for God does not annihilate our otherness – but by finding connections, relations, synergies and moving on.

Gone, then, are the days when members of one church family avoided contact with others, stressing only the doctrinal differences which separated them. Going, also, is the view of other faiths as godless otherness which may only be eliminated and replaced. Coming in its place is the comprehension that the omnipresent God has no barriers, and hence is 'with' them, as with us. That may be arrived at as a theological conclusion, but it surely resonates with witness and service in a pluralistic, multifaith, postmodern age.

What God, at home in change and variety, seeks is our lateral transcendence of set positions when these reduce our own mobility. On the other hand, these set positions have given the churches and all the people in them, their identity. It is not, therefore, a matter of simply departing from the status quo, 'going with the flow' in any or every way, which may be one of the excesses of postmodernity, but rather a case of not permitting the status quo to close doors on wider horizons and new possibilities. Transcendence of, say, Scottish Presbyterianism or English Methodism as they are now, does not necessarily mean leaving all of these behind, but rather seeing them in a new, potentially transforming light, as part of a larger interrelated, moving, changing whole, whose relations are all best defined by 'with'.

Thus far the lateral transcendence to relationship with others which I have been urging has had to do with humans in all their variety. But, finally, a relationship may be sought and found with the non-human others with whom we share this planet.

Citizens of modern Western nations pride themselves on their progressive social movements that touched the consciences of men in political power, moving them to free the slaves, give the vote to women, establish strong commitments to redressing centuries of injustice . . . However these leaders have great difficulty discovering the broader and deeper community of trees, rivers, mountains and animals. 'Giving the animals the vote' . . . is a metaphor used by the poet [Gary Snyder] to call our attention to the boundaries of community.[1]

Human and church response to the environment and its problems, problems which I will not describe here, as they have frequently been rehearsed already, runs at the moment from those who do not care, to the 'deep ecology' evidenced in this quotation, which wishes to insist on community with all of nature. It seems to me that while not everyone will wish to affirm the 'biocentric equality' of the deep ecologists, and the rather comfortable view of human liberation in the quotation, the concern of the churches will be nearer that end of the spectrum of response, which takes the natural world with full seriousness, than the one which is unmoved by the gravity of the situation.

Again theology underlies thought and action in this area, and I have described these at greater length in an earlier book.[2] A God who is omnipresent is present among the creatures of the Serengeti or the rainforests of Amazonia as well as among the human dwellers in cities and villages. And God was surely not absent from creation during all the aeons of evolution before humans arrived on the scene. There is therefore no reason to believe that God's care and attention are given only to human beings.

Further, God cannot be out of character. The constancy and unchangeableness of God is one of the pillars of the faith. So God's presence with non-human creatures is one of companionship, just as it is with humans. That conclusion has consequences. In the case of humans we believe that God knows our circumstances and possibilities, and understands us in the midst of these better than we do ourselves. So the same has to be said of God's understanding of other creatures. God knows intimately just how they are.

But a warning is worth repeating here. God must not be thought of like a human person observing the non-human from the outside. If the infinite God may understand finite humans as from within, then God may equally understand peacocks, boa-constrictors, nematodes and all the rest 'as from within'. Only humans, not God, are limited by the species barrier. To have to do with the natural world, then, is still to be interacting with what God cares for and accompanies.

In the first place that companionship may add to God's joy in the diversity of creation. But in the second place it means that God would know and suffer with creatures in the various ecological disasters which are scattered over our planet. For it is the same relation of companionship through good times and bad which exists between God and every non-human creature. It therefore matters to God how creatures are treated, and whether creation as a whole flourishes as best it can, or is put under considerable strain.

God, I have already argued, will not intervene to right ecological or any other wrongs, having given creation freedom to develop as it could. The degree to which that understanding is now accepted, however much intervention may be appealed to in more traditional ways, is shown in that no one, as far as I know, is beseeching God to change the composition of the upper atmosphere so that global warming will not take place. That is universally perceived as the result of human action, and its cure, if it comes, will also be the responsibility of human action.

From a theological point of view this is again right. Divine intervention on its own would remove the freedom and responsibility given to humans. Humans themselves, with their gift of freedom, are free to continue exploiting and exhausting stocks of creatures regarded as resources, but they are also free to turn around the worst effects of past actions. And since it is highly likely that God is concerned with the state of creation, concurrence will share that concern, and synergy with God will endeavour to work for its improvement. So, although God does not intervene, to the extent that humans perceive their responsibility, they, energized by and working with God may intervene to change what is going on, or to preserve a satisfactory state of natural being. This is something that churches could make clear to their members, that it is possible to be working with God for the good of creation.

But what character would this intervention or preservation take? It has seemed to many, both in and out of the churches, that stewardship is the answer. The Worldwide Fund for Nature, for instance, has set up a Stewardship

Project to feed into consideration of Land Reform in
Scotland. For churches the notion of stewardship is a familiar one, even if latterly it has been applied more to money
than to creatures. But there are frequent descriptions in the
Hebrew scriptures of humans having their power on earth
under a delegated authority from God, and being responsible
to God for its use. A Jewish comment on Genesis 1, for
example, expresses well the way in which this passage now
evokes in awakened sensibilities

> a real humility in which we see ourselves as part of the
> totality of Being, understand that nature itself is permeated
> with the spirit of God, and recognize that the chosenness
> of the human species, our ability to develop a certain level
> of consciousness, is at the same time an obligation towards
> compassion, caring, and stewardship.[3]

There is much to welcome in that statement, and in the
move to stewardship generally. Under its sway resources
would not simply be exhausted for short-term gain, as if their
existence or non-existence were of no consequence, nor
would the lives of fellow creatures be unnecessarily harsh or
diminished. Stewardship involves husbanding resources and
giving thought to the needs of future generations. Indeed it is
in humans' interest so to behave, for it is always possible that
some creature which would have become extinct under present practices will prove to have some characteristic which is
of benefit to humanity.

The armadillo is a good case in point. It was on the verge
of extinction when it was discovered that they are the only
creatures other than humans to suffer from leprosy. Further,
armadillos produce a reaction to leprosy from which a serum
has been made which cures leprosy in humans. Given that
there are still large tracts of the natural world to be explored
for such benefits it is folly on the part of humans to allow it
to be destroyed. So while

all living things on earth have some human reference and use, the proper human attitude is one of restraint, humility, and even non-interference, except for matters of necessity (such as daily bread).[4]

Thus Larry Rasmussen summarizes the benefits of stewardship. And indeed, if humans could reach such levels of self-restraint, much would be gained. But Rasmussen, like many others, draws attention to the implicit anthropocentrism (the elevation of humanity) of the model. The human is still the crown of creation, looking after the rest. The model does not do anything for the independently valuable status of the rest of creation in human or divine eyes. Human stewardship, moreover, is scarcely discernible from human management, which is far from the kind of relationship advocated in this book. It is a relation 'over' the rest, not 'with' them. Some relationships with domesticated animals or in decisions on land use may well have to have a considerable input of stewardship, but, I shall continue to argue, if that is all, there is something lacking in the attitude of church members to God's creation.

> Contemporary theology . . . provided the moral underpinnings for the ascendancy of man over nature which by the early modern period became the accepted goal of human endeavour. The dominant religious traditions had no truck with that 'veneration' of nature which many Eastern religions still retained and which the scientist Robert Boyle correctly recognized as 'a discouraging impediment to the empire of man over the inferior creatures'.
>
> K. Thomas, *Man and the Natural World*,
> Penguin 1984, p.22

The practice of companionship will not take place until and unless there is also the development of a fellow-feeling in general for our fellow creatures, that is, the perception of them as creatures like us, owing their existence to God, and also the recognition of them as our fellows, with their own interests in the planet we share. Reasons may be given for such a fellow-feeling, including the degree to which our own existence depends on their input – for clothes, food and shelter, and, more basically, for the clean air, unpolluted water and rich topsoil without which we could not survive. The environment is not, so to speak, 'out there', somewhere at a distance from humans who can look on at its tribulations. People are part of, taking from and contributing to, the whole which is the environment.

Although reasons may be given for human embeddedness in creation, reasons are not enough. Companionship is based on a belief that it is good that our fellow creatures should exist, and that it would be good that they exist even if humans were not there. They have their own independent and intrinsic value as what has evolved in creation, and as creatures which matter to God.

There is an arresting instance of what is almost a conversion to this appreciation of nature in Coleridge's 'Rime of the Ancient Mariner'. The seaman, cursed with the shot albatross round his neck, and having gone through various torments, watches some water snakes and enjoys their colours: 'Blue, glossy green and velvet black'. His attention is drawn away from himself and his plight to enjoy the independent existence of other creatures, and that leads him to bless them spontaneously:

> O happy living things! no tongue
> Their beauty might declare:
> A spring of love gush'd from my heart
> And I bless'd them unaware.

Immediately the albatross falls from the mariner's neck and his reinstatement, one might even say his resurrection, begins. He has come to value, even 'unaware', the natural world in its own right. Coleridge's conclusion may seem rather sentimentally expressed by modern standards, but it has a point.

> He prayeth best, who loveth best
> All things both great and small;
> For the dear God who loveth us,
> He made and loveth all.[5]

---

## The Optimistic View

'Ecology,' says one television commercial, 'is definitely in.' When even the pop culture makes such a pronouncement, when even that once-abstruse word ecology is now so familiar that it can be used in a commercial, the signs are favourable for environmentalists. The prevailing perception of the public mood in North America and elsewhere is that the public now generally recognizes the existence of an ecological crisis and is ready to respond earnestly . . . Some industrial giants are advertising themselves as sentimental caretakers of barn owl nestlings and wetland nurseries. Pollution-friendly politicians are hustling to remould their images as lifelong environmentalists.

J. Nash, *Loving Nature*, Abingdon 1991, p.17

---

*Pace* Coleridge, the valuing and sense of companionship with non-human nature is not merely a romantic attitude. It is easy (especially for town-dwellers) to believe that it is good that blackbirds and dragonflies and otters exist as our companion creatures, for they delight us, and we leave them alone. But farmers have a different view of their stock and crops, which could from time to time suffer from foot-rot or blight. And indeed we all have to eat our fellow creatures, and to control harmful species like mosquitos and the HIV virus. Here companionship blends with stewardship, but changes its tone. The difference companionship makes is in a basic respect for the lives of other creatures: giving a good life and an easy death to what will be eaten; and remaining aware, even as creatures noxious to humans or livestock are dealt with, that within creation this course is not an unqualified good, but the lesser of two evils.

Companionship will further insist on the moral standing of all creatures when their interests affect human decisions. There are certain goods which non-human creatures have, such as a safe habitat, a food supply, the possibility of mating and rearing young. To argue for the preservation of these is to present non-human creatures as morally considerable in, for instance, decisions on land use (such as whether wetlands are to remain a habitat or become a potential development site). As Stephen Clark has put it neatly: 'We should seek to act according to rules that allow all sorts of creatures a fair chance of living a life of their own choosing.'[6]

Companionship with the natural world is a further example of transcendence, in this case the transcendence of self-interest – having cheap food from factory farms on supermarket shelves, for example – and even human interest where it is impinging harmfully on fellow creatures. Transcendence like that does not expect a gift in exchange, a quid pro quo from the animals, say, for having done the decent thing by the non-human. Its rewards are in the implementation of its values and the enlarged sense of value it brings about.

Where companionship modifies the more managerial aspects of stewardship, and the sense that only humans matter, it will modify also all interaction with the natural world, from churchyards to green belts, from zoos to farms, from animal experimentation to genetic manipulation of crops and animals. Good information, of course, remains essential, to avoid the kind of foolishness which led people to 'liberate' mink from a farm, with the result that they died at large shortly after.

Much awareness of these issues has already appeared in churches; many, for instance, have replaced the traditional

## The Pessimistic View

Josef Vavrousek, Czech Minister of the Environment, at the 1991 meeting of European environment ministers:

Minister Vavrousek found little or no support for his proposals to create systematic pan-European agencies with power to formalize this new high water mark of awareness and concern about the ecological underpinnings of modern European society. He found no wish among environment ministers to go deeply into the ethical issues raised by the arrival of environmental concerns on the political agenda. There was instead a strong, if largely silent, desire to continue with business as usual, that is to say, the exercise of pragmatic flexibility.

Gwyn Prins, 'The Challenge of Ecology',
*True to the Earth* ed A. Race and R. Williamson,
Oneworld Publications 1995, p.17

Harvest Festival with a Festival of Creation. Martin Palmer has linked such celebration into the interfaith concern for the environment described in the last chapter:

We have asked the churches to invite people from a wide variety of religious and secular backgrounds, especially environmentalists, to celebrate the wonders of creation, and then within that to look not only at the destruction and abuse we have caused, but also at the potential for partnership between humanity and the rest of creation.[7]

This is an area of concern shared between the churches and many New Agers, sharing the values if not the theology. In that case, to see that the churches are serious on this issue would give them credibility where they currently lack it.

All versions of transcendence, however warily undertaken,

end in the transformation of perception. To church people who can transcend stereotypes and distrust, at least some New Agers become people of genuine values and concerns; people of other churches become fellow Christians; other faiths become fascinating accounts of how people have responded to a sense of God, or the Real; other creatures cease to be providentially useful resources for humans and become instead creation in its full and resounding sense of which we are a part.

At the same time the self-understanding of the churches changes. From being primarily a continuation of the past a church becomes a response to the present. From being concerned with form and order it becomes concerned with the widest possible relationships. From enshrining where God was, it puts hope and synergy into where it perceives God now.

# 13

# The Church as Ark,
# the Church as Salt

The church has always subsisted under a variety of metaphors. Paul Minear, for instance, found ninety-six in the New Testament, and more have been added since. Minear enjoyed this superfluity, and in his conclusion regretted the way in which certain central metaphors, originally spun by the visionary creative imagination, hardened over time into dogma. At that point the implications of the metaphors came to be applied to the church as the implications of dogma with a literalness never originally in view. That may be seen in the way the church used to define itself over against heretics. Only those the church accepted as such could be the People of God or the Body of Christ. Others were not on the same pilgrimage (headed in the right direction), or would die spiritually outside the tightly-knit body. The positiveness and elasticity of the figures of speech had gone, let alone what Minear called 'the primal communal experience' which gave rise to the metaphors in the first place.[1]

Later, when different metaphors came to be adopted, different ecclesial cultures arose round them. And while every metaphor has its positive side in giving a self-definition to the church, no metaphor can encompass everything, so every dominant one will have its limitations. Thus the church conceived as Rock may have strength, endurance and offer shelter, but it is not easily going to see itself as the subject of historical contingency and change, nor is it going to be responsive to cultural differences.

Another church may take as central the Word of God,

which is not simply a reference to the Bible, but extends into christological and ecclesiastical beliefs and practices, including building a church like an auditorium with a central pulpit. The flexibility of the verbal metaphor has been great, but with its (in its own way admirable) emphasis on understanding it has had little place for experience and feeling, and with its primacy of the verbal it has not cultivated the visually aesthetic or exciting, though these, at the same time, have their own dangers. But it is thus at a disadvantage in a visual culture.

Even the recent, attractive notion of the church as sacrament, enacting and mediating divine grace through mutual interaction, has its limitations. Only if God's grace is understood not to be confined to what the church is and does will the implemented metaphor avoid the charge of separating off too easily a holy church from an unholy world which it alone may supply with divine grace. Further,

> it remains true that sacramentalism, carried to excess, can induce an attitude of narcissistic aestheticism that is not easily reconcilable with a full Christian commitment to social and ethical values.[2]

Not surprisingly, Minear disliked the move from metaphor to dogma, and recommended the return to the imaginative holding of many metaphors.

> Such a restoration of the Christian imagination may enable the church to use again the whole medley of New Testament images with an authentic comprehension of their meaning, freed from the idolatry and tyranny of words.[3]

In a similar, but unrelated, move, Ian Ramsey once recommended that many models for divine activity should be entertained simultaneously to prevent any single one from becoming dominant and potentially harmful.[4]

But these prescriptions, attractive as they are, seem impossible to follow. Against Minear one might argue that a church growing in numbers and requiring some organization and settled teaching for all could not be content to dwell in metaphors for ever. Apart from anything else, not every member of the church is imaginative. I was once describing the symbolism of church building to a group of Scottish elders, concluding with a round church as the symbol of fellowship. Their only reaction? 'Very poor acoustics in a round building.' That may be true, but it is hardly an imaginative response. Against Ramsey one could argue that the simultaneous *equal* entertainment of a number of metaphors, which will be variously incompatible, is impossible. In an almost evolutionary way one will come to dominate and make a single coherent picture, and then dictate priorities.

Taking these difficulties on board, but still wishing to use metaphors to give a sense of the church, I propose two that are very different. So long as they are both held in view, and there are enough people in a democratic church who lean towards one more than the other, both may perhaps be kept alive. And the existence of the other would keep each from dictating the church's being on its own with the inevitable consequent constriction. Thus each may save the church from the excesses of the other.

The first proposal is the church as ark, a structured, organized container vessel. There has been little in this book hitherto on the value of tradition, structure, organization. The reason for that is not hard to find. No church that I have encountered, in Britain or at the WCC, has not been aware that it carries a tradition, and that it requires a structure to continue that tradition. Even the Pentecostalists of Latin America – and of Britain – are developing traditions and structures as one generation succeeds another. Churches of any length of history do not have to be persuaded of their character as ark, as carrying through their own times the inheritance from the past, in order to hand it on to future generations.

Certainly the church has always required some organization, ever since Paul complained that the Corinthians were obscuring the gospel by their undisciplined behaviour (I Cor.14). Avery Dulles remarks on its necessity:

> Throughout its history, from its very earliest years, Christianity has always had an institutional side. It has recognized ministers, accepted confessional formulas, prescribed forms of public worship. All this is fitting and proper.[5]

And indeed it has been. The problem, as Dulles recognizes, is 'institutionalism', 'a system in which the institutional element is treated as primary'. His word 'treated' is important, for institutionalized churches do not *describe* themselves as such, they just *behave* as such. Most churches probably have some people in this mould, probably in positions of institutional power, who want things done, not only 'decently and in order' as Paul recommended to the Corinthians (I Cor.14.40), but in the particular order which has been in place for generations, which has given the church its character and which, people would argue, has blessed the church heretofore.

Two examples of the excess of institutionalism in relation to the church as ark will make the point of its self-concern and unwillingness to entertain challenge. Rahner, amazingly candid as he often is, declares:

> Office-holders and clerics particularly are liable to become ecclesiastical introverts. They think of the church, not of people. They want to see the church free, but not human beings. Under National Socialism, for instance, we thought considerably more about ourselves and about upholding what belonged to the church and its institutions, than about the fate of the Jews.[6]

In relation to my own Church of Scotland I have been haunted by a sentence of Harry Whitley's: 'The certified

soundness of dull men had triumphed.'[7] That is his concluding remark on the nineteenth-century trial of Edward Irving
who had encouraged 'the gifts of the Spirit' in his congregations, and had argued that Christ was not born incapable of
sin. The issue here was as much theological as to do with
order, but 'the certified soundness of dull men', 'certified' by
the institutional framework of the church, may reinforce any
of the current aspects.

---

### The Slow Route

The fact that church leaders are, generally speaking,
averse to change is not in itself theologically significant.
This has been the case ever since Christianity was adopted
in the fourth century as the established religion of the
Roman Empire... It is the recognized role of ecclesiastical
rulers to conserve the inheritance of the past. This is an
important and necessary role, worthy of respect. But it is
also necessary that there be others who explore new paths
of thought in the ever-changing human situation. And
when ... after long discussion . . . and gradually producing incremental shifts in outlook, a new consensus eventu-
ally emerges, the official leadership will then endorse it,
and it will be orthodoxy!

J. Hick, *The Rainbow of Faiths*, SCM Press 1995, p.133

---

The ark may be in many ways a splendid old ship, for
which one may give thanks, for it brought the gospel to us
all. But it also may be pictured as an ancient, creaking, over-
burdened vessel, more concerned to keep itself seaworthy
than anything else. Puns are possible. The ark is arcane,
holding within it antique mysteries inaccessible to all but the
initiates. The ark is archive, bearing the huge weight of the
records of the past – doctrines, canon law, books of order,
ecclesiastical histories – impeding its progress. (Today,
perhaps, one might hope for the ark as archipelago, a series

of communities making one whole.) On the other hand, however, the ark is still there, and its capacity for enduring, for connecting the present with the past, and possibly sailing into the future, is, perhaps, its most persuasive feature.

But its limitations are also in evidence. Apart from its sclerotic tendencies in a rapidly changing world, 'it is all too easy to reduce our vision of the church to something we can control', writes Robin Greenwood.[8] Institutions exist to make such control more manageable, and that is equally true of church institutions. But with that control comes implicitly the control of God whose energies within any church are limited by its boundaries. Reinhold Niebuhr saw this danger and inveighed against it:

> To be turned towards God and to be converted to the church becomes almost identical; the way to God is through the church . . . God is almost defined as the one who is encountered in the church, or the one in whom the church believes.[9]

These are serious limitations. Yet change is risky, and hearts may fail at its insecurity. John Bell links that with the insecurity of the Israelites who, having left Egypt, found themselves wandering in a desert.

> Moses has to counteract the majority of desert pilgrims who, rather than thank God for past deliverance and trust God for the future, raise their voices in the reactionary jibe: '*Back to Egypt*' (Numbers 14.3).
>
> There is a back-to-Egypt brigade in every congregation, and there is a back-to-Egypt corner in every soul, as in the face of uncertainties ahead of us we retreat into selective reminiscing about the halcyon days which never really were.[10]

But, for all its insecurity, what I have been urging in this book is that *present* responsiveness to *present* situations is the prime responsibility of the church, and that it is our responsiveness, our capacity for synergy, which matters to God now, not the history of our past, nor the efficiency of our organization. A responsive church may be described under the metaphor of salt. Whereas the ark gathers people into itself, salt must go to where it is needed, and where its possibilities lie. It, therefore, has much more need to be thoroughly acquainted with the present situation than does the church as ark, which fundamentally needs to know only its own situation and the weather it is likely to run into. Salt is a lively, extrovert metaphor. It is no good in heaps, and loses its flavour-enhancing power if it is stored.

'You are the salt of the earth,' Jesus says to the crowds in Matthew 5.13, and salt has to have its effect now or not at all. Its evanescence is underlined: 'if salt has lost its taste, how can its saltiness be restored?' For the church under the metaphor of salt it is today's encounters and what will make them effective that matters. But salt is sprinkled, it cannot be applied in a thick coating like breadcrumbs, and that is a good reminder of the light and sensitive touch needed today:

Being salt . . . A major project over the last year has been a link with the local tenants' association. Some people have asked when we hope to take over the running of the group and to make it 'Christian', but this is to misunderstand our intentions. We are open about our faith, but our first role is to serve the community by being available for advice, counselling or transport and by providing workers for their summer play scheme and after-school club. It has been especially exciting when children, parents and members of the committee have then come along to one of our services. In an area where social churchgoing is certainly not the norm, and many people have been put off by conventional expressions of religion, it is important that we are seen by others as practical people who genuinely care, who can be trusted.[11]

The church as salt, however, is also about the saltiness of the community itself. Without that, there is nothing to carry into the world. That is the emphasis Konrad Raiser gives to the metaphor, playing up the purifying and preserving characteristics of salt.

What is at stake here is the role of the Christian community in and for the world. It can assume this role only if it does not dissolve and disappear, but remains recognizable as salt, as that which consecrates the covenant of life and which preserves and purifies ... The Christian community as 'salt of the earth' is thus more than just the 'religious component' in the general flavour of the culture. Its function is critical, even aggressive, in the sense of preventing disintegration, decay and rottenness; and it is positive in the sense of being a healing, purifying force which re-establishes the links of fellowship in a community.[12]

> Let us be like salt in the ocean,
>     giving salt to all humanity.
> Help people know the holy taste of the Lord
>     and his living breath receive.
>
> Let us all care and love one another,
>     removing hatred and evil from our midst.
> Ask the Lord to unite our hearts and wills
>     and to all peoples happiness bring.
>
> C. H. Kao, *Testimonies of Faith:*
> *Letters and Poems from Prison in Taiwan,*
> Study 5, World Alliance of Reformed Churches

So the effects of salt are internal, being concerned with how each community *is*, with a ministry and organization which, so to speak, promote salt, and also external, changing the taste of life for those who will receive it. In the process, as Greenwood notes, the church itself will change:

> Would it not be more according to the mind of Jesus if we dared to concentrate on the quality of our church community's inner life and worked at becoming good salt, and light that really sheds illumination? The church that emerges from this kind of approach may not easily be recognized. It may have to part company with buildings, status and an easy moralistic answer to theological and moral dilemmas.[13]

It is the church as salt, not the church as ark, that will connect most with postmodern, pluralistic, multifaith Britain. I have proposed a church of small, diverse communities, with a wider range of ministry and participation, internally cohesive with shared interests such as spirituality or environmental concern, and externally linked by networks of relationship, including ecumenical relationship. Such a church will be no less Christian for being open to dialogue with, and discovery from, other faiths. If that came to pass it would intensify what is going on already here and there into the church's perceived and avowed persona and self-understanding in terms of synergy with God. Yet Victor de Waal's comment remains true:

> But the difficulty is, of course, that every idea, if it is to be socially effective, *has* to be institutionally incorporated. And every institution, even any group, is bound to create its tradition, its mythology, its frame of reference.[14]

So salt cannot escape the tendency to become ark. The question then becomes how the two can coexist without damage to the salt. At the moment the institution has the power of decision-making in the churches, and the change will have to come from there.

The church, like any other institution in human society, is tempted, as was Jesus himself, to hold on to what it has, to safeguard itself, but this temptation must be resisted and the church must be prepared and willing to die ... The church indeed may be regarded as the first-fruits, but it must not be forgotten that that is also a sacrificial term (Lev.2.12; Rom.11.16).[15]

Those who wish the church to be more like salt would have to make a concerted effort to persuade the decision-makers, by showing them what exists (that is, actually giving them 'hands on' awareness of contemporary contexts), describing what is possible, advertising, in all senses of the word, their vision for the church. Nothing will happen unless the experience of critical people within the church is changed, and unless considerable noise and explanation is undertaken. For in the end nothing will change unless the institutional element in the church permits, endorses and indeed promotes considerable experimentation, without being too worried over whether these cohere with past practice or the church's public profile. (It may, in fact, be difficult to persuade the media that change is happening, for they also have a fixed idea of what the church is and what it stands for – mostly moral denunciation.)

Then there would have to be self-denial on the part of the institution, won over to, or at least going along with, the perception of the priority of present responsiveness over past structures. Among other things it would need to allow: a great diminution of ecclesiastical bureaucracy; a tolerance of diversity; agreement for responsibility taken and decisions made at local level with plenty of lay participation and lay leadership, with pastoral care.

In the end, the amount of ark-character, of institution, that any church needs, is only enough to see that there will be salt in this and future generations. The ark exists for the sake of the salt, not the other way round. And a salt-bearing, salt-spreading ark will be quite a humble vessel.

First of all we must recognize soberly that no planning of the church's future in the next decades can relieve us of the necessity of going forward into a future that cannot be planned, of risk, of danger and of hope in the incalculable grace of God.

K. Rahner, *The Shape of the Church to Come*, SPCK 1974, p.45

# Notes

Part One: God with Us

1. *Then and Now*

1. V. de Waal, *What is the Church?*, SCM Press 1969; R. Adolfs, *The Grave of God*, Burns and Oates 1967.
2. de Waal, op. cit., p.20.
3. Adolfs, op. cit., p.119.
4. D. McCrone, 'The Postmodern Condition of Scottish Society', *The Future of the Kirk: Theology in Scotland*, Occasional Paper 2, March 1997, p.12.
5. K. Rahner, *The Shape of the Church to Come*, SPCK 1974, p.82.
6. H. Hunke, 'Churches and Faith Organizations on the Internet', *Echoes*, Programme Unit III Publications, WCC, December 1997, p.29.
7. L. Dawson and J.Henneby, 'New Religions and the Internet', *Journal of Contemporary Religion*, Vol. 14, No. l, January 1999, p.33.
8. Cf. L. Dawson, 'Who Joins New Religious Movements and Why: Twenty Years of Research and What Have we Learned?', *Studies in Religion*, 25(2), pp. 193-213.
9. A.Wimberley, 'Called to Listen: the Imperative Vocation of Listening in Twenty-first Century Faith Communities', *International Review of Mission*, July 1998, p.340.

2. *God-with*

1. E. Jüngel, *The Doctrine of the Trinity: God's Being is in Becoming*, Scottish Academic Press 1976, p.106.
2. I have described this at greater length in *Ambiguity and the Presence of God*, SCM Press 1985, pp.135-39.
3. J.A T. Robinson, *On Being the Church in the World*, SCM Press 1960, p.56.

4. K. Rahner, *Nature and Grace*, Sheed and Ward 1963, p.25.
5. M. Northcott, Introduction to 'Work in the City', *Urban Theology* ed M. Northcott, Cassell 1998, p.195.
6. Rahner, *Nature and Grace*, p.22.
7. A. Primavesi, *Sacred Gaia*, Routledge, forthcoming 2000.
8. Cf. H. LaFollette, *Personal Relationships: Love, Identity and Morality*, Blackwell 1996, ch.1.
9. See, e.g., in R. Frost, *Selected Poems*, Penguin 1978, p.48.
10. J. McLeod Campbell, *The Nature of the Atonement* (1855), Macmillan and Co. 1895.
11. P. Tillich, *The Shaking of the Foundations*, SCM Press 1949; Penguin 1962, p.163.
12. D.W Winnicott, *The Maturational Processes and the Facilitation Environment: Studies in the Theory of Emotional Development*, Hogarth Press 1965, pp.37-55.
13. D.W. Winnicott, *Playing and Reality*, Tavistock Publications 1971.
14. R. Page, *God and the Web of Creation*, SCM Press 1996, pp.5-12.
15. J. Moltmann, *The Church in the Power of the Spirit*, SCM Press 1977, p.116.
16. Ibid., p.118.
17. K. Rahner, *The Christian Commitment*, Sheed and Ward 1963, p.47.
18. J. Moltmann, *The Open Church*, SCM Press 1978, p.61.
19. R. Page, *Ambiguity and the Presence of God*, pp. 188-216.
20. R. Page, *The Incarnation of Freedom and Love*, SCM Press 1991, *passim*.
21. Page, *Ambiguity and the Presence of God*, p.197.
22. Ibid., p.195.
23. Ibid., p.194.

## 3. *Us-with*

1. K. Rahner, *The Shape of the Church to Come*, SPCK 1974, pp.21f.
2. J. A.T. Robinson, *The Body: a Study in Pauline Theology*, SCM Press 1952, p.7; *On Being the Church in the World*, SCM Press 1960, pp.26f.
3. M. Palmer, *Coming of Age: An Exploration of Christianity and the New Age*, The Aquarian Press (HarperCollins) 1993, p.40.
4. A. Dulles, *Models of the Church*, Gill and Macmillan, 2nd edn 1988, p.163.
5. P. Minear, *Images of the Church in the New Testament*, Lutterworth Press 1961.

6. Rahner, *The Shape of the Church to Come*, p.43.

7. W. Storrar, 'Understanding the Silent Disruption', *The Future of the Kirk: Theology in Scotland*, Occasional Paper 2, March 1997, p.21-36.

8. Storrar, art. cit., p.23.

9. J. Tiller, 'The Associational Church and its Communal Mission', *Urban Theology: A Reader* ed M. Northcott, Cassell 1998, p.277.

10. D. Green, *Reinventing Civil Society*, IEA Health and Welfare Unit 1993, p.131.

11. M. Kane, *What Kind of God?*, SCM Press 1986, p.120.

12. L McSpadden, 'Foreword', W. Wink, *Healing a Nation's Wounds*, Life and Peace Institute, Uppsala 1996, p.iv.

13. W. Ariarajah, *Gospel and Culture: ongoing discussion within the ecumenical movement*, WCC Publications 1987, p.9.

14. Ibid., pp.11,13.

15. D. Paton, *Breaking Barriers: Nairobi 1975*, WCC/SPCK/Eerdmans 1976, p.78.

16. J. Pobee, *West Africa: Christ Would be an African Too*, WCC 1996, pp.51f.

17. D. Bosch, *Transforming Mission: Paradigm Shifts in Theology of Mission*, Orbis Books 1991, p.367.

18. R Greenwood, *Reclaiming the Church*, Collins Fount 1988, p.24. Cf. J. Sepulveda, *The Andean Highlands: an encounter with two forms of Christianity*, WCC 1997; A Davidson, *Aotearoa-New Zealand: defining moments in the gospel-culture encounter*, WCC 1996.

19. W Storrar, *Scottish Identity: A Christian Vision*, The Handsel Press 1990, p.165.

20. Dulles, op.cit., p.71.

21. R. Page, *Ambiguity and the Presence of God*, SCM Press 1985, pp.54-61.

22. K. Rawls, 'Philosophy and the Environmental Movement', *Spirit of the Environment* eds D.Cooper and J. Palmer, Routledge 1998, p.139.

23. R. Wiliams, 'Hegel and the gods of postmodernity', *Shadow of Spirit: Postmodernism and Religion* ed P. Berry and A. Wemick, Routledge 1992, p.72.

24. L. Boeve, 'Market and Religion in Postmodern Culture', *Theology*, January-February 1999, p.32.

25. Ibid., p.33.

26. A. Gare, *Postmodernism and the Environmental Crisis*, Routledge 1995, p.139.

27. Ibid., p.140

28. Boeve, art.cit., p.35.

29. Gare, ibid.
30. Boeve, ibid.


4. *Withness*

1. I. Bria, *Romania: Orthodox Identity at the Crossroads of Europe*, WCC Publications 1995, pp.33f.
2. K. Rahner, *Theological Investigations*, Vol. IV, Darton, Longman and Todd 1966, p.167 .
3. 'Toward a Common Understanding of the Church', *Catholic International*, September 1991, p.790.
4. Rahner, op.cit., p.180.
5. D. Bosch, *Transforming Mission*, Orbis Books 1991, p.485.

## Part Two: Synergy in the Church

### 5. *Synergy involves Change*

1. A. Hastings, *The Theology of a Protestant Catholic*, SCM Press 1990, p.38.
2. K. Rahner, *The Shape of the Church to Come*, SPCK 1974, p.24.
3. J. Segundo, *The Community Called Church*, Gill and Macmillan 1980, p.48.
4. V. Donovan, *The Church in the Midst of Creation*, SCM Press 1989.
5. D. Bosch, *Transforming Mission*, Orbis Books 1991, p.294.
6. J. Scherer, *Gospel, Church and Kingdom: Comparative Studies in World Mission Theology*, Augsburg 1987, p.77.
7. Donovan, op.cit., p.37.
8. Ibid., p.46.
9. Report of the Assembly Council to the General Assembly of the Church of Scotland 1998, 3.1.2.
10. Donovan, op.cit., p.46.
11. Ibid., p.47.
12. K. Raiser, *To be the Church: Challenges and Hopes for the New Millenium*, WCC Publications 1997, p.7.
13. E. Patey, *Faith in a Risk-Taking God*, Darton, Longman and Todd 1991, p.9.
14. K. Barth, *Church Dogmatics*, IV/1, T & T Clark 1965, p.653.
15. A. Hastings, op.cit., p.45.
16. J. Moltmann, *The Church in the Power of the Spirit*, SCM Press 1977, p.290.

## 6. Community and its Ministry

1. A. Hake, 'Theological Reflections on Community', *Theology in the City* ed. A. Harvey, SPCK 1989, p.47.
2. J. Vanier, *From Brokenness to Community*, Paulist Press 1992, p.16.
3. Ibid.
4. Ibid., p.17.
5. *Gaudium et spes*, 40, 17 December 1965.
6. R. Greenwood, *Reclaiming the Church*, Collins Fount 1988, p.48.
7. Ibid., p.46.
8. K. Popper, *The Open Society and its Enemies*, Vol. 2, Routledge 1966, p.237.
9. J. Calvin, *Institutes of the Christian Religion*, IV.iii.1.
10. Greenwood, op.cit., p.172.
11. Ibid., p.127.
12. Ibid.
13. J. Moltmann, *The Church in the Power of the Spirit*, SCM Press 1977, p.246.
14. A. Hastings, *The Theology of a Protestant Catholic*, SCM Press 1990, p.141.
15. E. Patey, *Faith in a Risk-Taking God*, Darton Longman and Todd 1991, p.124.
16. Ibid., p.112.
17. A. Morisy, *Beyond the Good Samaritan: Community, Ministry and Mission*, Mowbray 1997, p.49; reprinted as 'Praxis, prayer and liturgy in a secular world' in *Urban Theology: A Reader* ed M. Northcott, Cassell 1998, p.238. This *Reader* is an extremely useful source of several of the pieces quoted.
18. N. Bradbury, *City of God? Pastoral Care in the Inner City*, SPCK 1989, p.68; reprinted as 'A Worshipping Community' in *Urban Theology*, p.245.
19. A. Hastings, op.cit., p.73.
20. Morisy, op.cit., p.58; art. cit., p.243.
21. D. Thomas, 'Community Work and Community Development', unpublished paper cited in *Church and Community Work*, Church of England Board for Social Responsibility 1988, p.6.
22. *Mission Statements: a book of practical ideas for ministry by the whole people of God*, The Association of Scottish Community Ministers, n.d, p.84.
23. *Church and Community Work*, pp. 6f.
24. Ibid., p.8.
25. J. Moltmann, *The Crucified God*, SCM Press 1974.
26. K. Pound, 'Training for Collaborative Ministry' in *Collaborative*

*Ministry: working together in collaborative style*, British Council of Churches 1987, p.11.

27. D. Gardner in *Collaborative Ministry*, p.22.
28. *The Sign we Give*, Report from the Working Party on Collaborative Ministry, Catholic Bishops' conference of England and Wales, Matthew Jones Publishing 1995.
29. Gardner, art. cit., p.25.
30. M. Grundy, *Understanding Congregations*, Mowbray 1998, pp.65-70.
31. J. McKay, *This Small Pool*, Trinity St Mungo Press 1997, p.36.
32. Ibid., pp.21f.
33. R. Page, *Theology and Industrial Mission*, Scottish Churches Industrial Mission 1994, p.2.
34. J. Monks, 'Modernising the Trade Union Movement', *AUT Bulletin*, January 1996, p.5.
35. R. Page, op.cit., p.13.

## 7. *Postmodern Spirituality*

1. M. Palmer, *Coming of Age*, The Aquarian Press (Harper/Collins) 1993, p.169.
2. Ibid., p.42.
3. J. Drane, *What is the New Age Saying to the Church?*, Marshall Pickering 1991, p.53.
4. Ibid., p.234.
5. M. Palmer, 'Faith, the Churches and European Unification', *Christian Values in Europe* ed G. Davies, R. Gill, and S. Pattison, 1993, p.15.
6. Drane, op. cit., p.205.
7. Ibid., p.14.
8. M. Palmer, *Coming of Age*, p.146.
9. D. Bosch, *Transforming Mission*, Orbis Books 1991, p.355.
10. M. Palmer, op cit., p.189.
11. Ibid., p.190.
12. N. Davies, *Wales: Language, Nation, Faith and Witness*, WCC Publications 1996, p.33.
13. A. Langerak, 'Ecumenical Letter on Evangelism', WCC, July 1999.
14. J.G. Davies, *Worship and Mission*, SCM Press 1966, p.41.
15. T. Merton, *Life and Holiness*, Doubleday Image Books 1964, p.103.
16. J. Bell, *States of Bliss and Yearning: the marks of authentic Christian spirituality*, Wild Goose Publications 1998, pp.10f.
17. T. Merton, *Contemplation in a World of Action*, Mandala Books (Unwin Paperbacks) 1980, p.158.

18. E. de Waal, *The Celtic Vision: prayers and blessings from the Outer Hebrides*, Darton, Longman and Todd 1988, pp.4f.

19. A. Allchin, *The World is a Wedding: Explorations in Christian Spirituality*, Darton, Longman and Todd 1988, pp.56, 51.

20. S. McFague, *The Body of God: An Ecological Theology*, SCM Press 1993, p.49.

21. S. McFague, *Models of God: Theology for an Ecological, Nuclear Age*, SCM Press 1987, pp.71 ,74.

22. K. Rahner, *Grace in Freedom*, Burns and Oates 1969, pp.127f.

## 8. *Peace and Justice*

1. J.K. Galbraith, 'Towards a new world deal', *The Guardian*, 26 June 1994.

2. N. Postman, *Amusing Ourselves to Death: Public Discourse in the Age of Show Business*, Penguin Books 1985, pp.viif.

3. J. Moltmann, *The Church in the Power of the Spirit*, SCM Press 1977, p.79.

4. D. Forrester and D. Skene, *Just Sharing*, Epworth Press 1988, p.63; reprinted as 'Love, Justice and Sharing: a Christian Perspective' in *Urban Theology: A Reader* ed M. Northcott, Cassell 1998, p.113.

5. M. Walsh, 'Organizing for Action', *Urban Theology*, p.135.

6. Ibid., p.137

7. K. David, *Sacrament and Struggle: Signs and instruments of grace from the downtrodden*, WCC Publications 1994, p.6.

8. G. Wheale, 'The Parish and Politics' in *Church and Politics* ed G. Moyser, T & T Clark 1985, p.153; reprinted in *Urban Theology*, p.150.

9. R. Greenwood, *Reclaiming the Church*, Collins Fount 1988, p.167.

10. Ibid.

11. J. Segundo, *The Community called Church: a theology for a new humanity*, Gill and Macmillan 1980, p.102.

12. Emma Leslie, untitled contribution in *The Landmines Campaign Still Needs the Churches*, LWF/WARC/WCC 1998.

13. *Fifty Years and More*, Programme Unit Four, Sharing and Service, WCC 1995.

## 9. *Ecumenism*

1. *Toward a Common Understanding of the Church*, Report on Reformed-Roman Catholic Dialogue 1984-1990, 1.4.63.

2. Frank Wright, 'The Reconciliation of Memories', *Northern Ireland: a Challenge to Theology*, Centre for Theology and Public Issues, University of Edinburgh 1987, p.56.
3. *Sixth Report* of the Joint Working Group between the Roman Catholic Church and the WCC, WCC Publications 1990, p.41.
4. *The Dublin Agreed Statement*, SPCK 1984, p.15.
5. Cf. 'Directory for the Application of Principles and Norms in Ecumenism', 25 March 1993.
6. A. Hastings, *The Theology of a Protestant Catholic*, SCM Press 1990, p.8.
7. Ibid., p.86.
8. L. Sanneh, 'Theological Method in Cultural Analysis', *International Review of Mission*, January-April 1995, p.59.
9. Hastings, op.cit., p.87.
10. E. Patey, *Faith in a Risk-taking God*, Darton, Longman and Todd 1991, p.63.
11. Consultation Report, 'Renewal out of Africa', *Ministerial Formation*, No.71, October 1995, p.6.
12. K. Raiser, *To be the Church*, WCC Publications 1997, p.77
13. See A. Wessels, *Europe: Was it Ever Really Christian?*, SCM Press 1994.
14. K. Raiser, op.cit., p.59.
15. H. Küng, *The Church*, Search Press 1968, p.304.
16. Ibid., p.355.

## 10. Mission

1. J. Moltmann, *The Church in the Power of the Spirit*, SCM Press 1977, p.65.
2. D. Bosch, *Transforming Mission*, Orbis Books 1990, p.519.
3. L. Turnipseed, 'Turning to God: Missional Responses in the Changing US Context', *International Review of Mission*, October 1998, p.530.
4. D. Bosch, op.cit., p.392.
5. J Brown, 'Situation Report on Eastern Europe', *International Review of Mission*, July 1997, p.314.
6. C. Palm, 'Toward a World Mission Tribunal', *International Review of Mission*, July 1997, p.298.
7. S. W. Park, 'A Survey of Mission Work in the Korean Churches, *International Review of Mission*, July 1997, p.333.
8. L. Boff, *Liberating Grace*, Orbis Books 1984, p.73.
9. J. Oman, *Vision and Authority*, 2nd edn Hodder 1928, p.308.
10. Ibid., p.312.
11. Ibid., p.313.

12. M. Bermudez, 'Sent in the Spirit to announce good news: a testimony of grassroots ministry in Costa Rica', *International Review of Mission*, October 1998, p.515.
13. E. Smith, *Mandate for Mission*, Friendship Press 1968, p.71.
14. Bosch, op.cit., p.296.
15. J. Mugambi, 'A Fresh Look at Evangelism in Africa', *International Review of Mission*, July 1998, p.344.
16. Ibid., p.346.
17. J.-M. EIa, *African City*, Orbis Books 1986, p.119.
18. C. Geffré, 'Christianity and Culture', *International Review of Mission*, January-April 1995, p.22.
19. Ibid., pp.27, 30.
20. 'Restructuring of Churches for Mission', *International Review of Mission*, July 1997, p.241.

11. *Other Faiths*

1. J. Hick, *The Rainbow of Faiths: Critical Dialogues on Religious Pluralism*, SCM Press 1995, p.125.
2. R. Drummond, *Toward a New Age in Christian Theology*, Orbis Books 1984, p.195.
3. D. Bosch, *Transforming Mission*, Orbis Books 1990, p.484.
4. J. Hick, op.cit. p.111.
5. K. Ward, *A Vision to Pursue: Beyond the Crisis in Christianity*, SCM Press 1991, p.190.
6. *Nostra Aetate*, 2,3, 28 October 1965.
7. H. Küng, *On Being a Christian*, Collins 1977; SCM Press 1991, p.98.
8. D. Bosch, op.cit., p.481.
9. K. Rahner, *Nature and Grace*, Sheed and Ward 1963, p.31.
10. G. Khodr, 'Christanity in a Pluralistic World - The Economy of the Holy Spirit', *Ecumenical Review*, April 1971 pp.118f.
11. W. Ariarajah, *The Bible and People of other Faiths*, WCC Publications 1994, p.31.
12. Ibid., p.67.
13. Ibid., p.68.
14. Ibid.
15. Bosch, op.cit., p.485.
16. Hick, op. cit., p.122.
17. C. Geffré, 'Mission Issues in the Contemporary Context of Multifaith Situations', *International Review of Mission*, July 1997, p.408.
18. 'The EATWOT Consultation on Religion and Liberation, New Delhi', *Ecumenical Review*, January 1989, p.124.

19. J. Esposito, *The Islamic Threat: Myth or Reality?*, OUP 1992, p.14.
20. A. Race, 'Faith in the Faiths', *True to this Earth: Global Changes and Transforming Faith* ed A. Race and R. Williamson, Oneworld Publications 1998, p.154.
21. M. Palmer, *Coming of Age*, The Aquarian Press (HarperCollins) 1993, p.154.
22. Ibid., p.78.

## 12. *The Environment*

1. B. Devall, *Simple in Means, Rich in Ends: Practising Deep Ecology*, Green Print 1990, p.191.
2. R. Page, *God and the Web of Creation*, SCM Press 1996.
3. M. Lerner, *Jewish Renewal: A Path to healing and Transformation*, Putnam 1995, p.416.
4. L. Rasmussen, *Earth Community, Earth Ethics*, WCC Publications 1996, p.231.
5. Samuel Taylor Coleridge (1772-1834), *The Rime of the Ancient Mariner*, parts iv, vii.
6. S. Clark, *How to Think about the Earth: Philosophical and Theological Models for Ecology*, Mowbray 1993, p.115.
7. M. Palmer, *Coming of Age*, The Aquarian Press (HarperCollins) 1993, p.189.

## 13. *The Church as Ark, the Church as Salt*

1. P. Minear, *Images of the Church in the New Testament*, Lutterworth Press 1961, p.252.
2. A. Dulles, *Models of the Church*, Gill and Macmillan, 2nd edn 1988, p.75.
3. P. Minear, op.cit., p.267.
4. I. Ramsey, *Models for Divine Activity*, SCM Press 1973.
5. A. Dulles, op.cit., p.35.
6. K. Rahner, *The Shape of the Church to Come*, SPCK 1974, p.61.
7. H. Whitley, *Blinded Eagle: An Introduction to the Life and Teaching of Edward Irving*, SCM Press 1955.
8. R. Greenwood, *Reclaiming the Church*, Collins Fount 1988, p.168.
9. R. Niebuhr, *Radical Monotheism and Western Culture*, Scribner's 1961, p.59.
10. J. Bell, *States of Bliss and Yearning*, Wild Goose Publications 1998, p.20.

11. H. Bonnick, 'Plaistow Christian Fellowship' in *Ten Inner City Churches* ed Michael Easton, MARC Europe 1988, p.191; reprinted in *Urban Theology: A Reader* ed M. Northcott, Cassell 1998, p.292.

12. K. Raiser, *To be the Church*, WCC Publications 1997, p.47.

13. Greenwood, op.cit., p.51.

14. V. de Waal, *What is the Church?*, SCM Press 1969, p.81.

15. J. Davies, *Worship and Mission*, SCM Press 1956, p.51.

# Index of Subjects

# Index of Names